THE BIG
Football Collection
ROB CHILDS

including
THE BIG GAME • THE BIG MATCH • THE BIG PRIZE

WITHDRAWN
FROM STOCK

YOUNG CORGI BOOKS

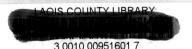

THE BIG FOOTBALL COLLECTION
A YOUNG CORGI BOOK : 9780552542975

PRINTING HISTORY
This collection first published 1995
Copyright © 1995 by Rob Childs

13 15 17 19 20 18 16 14 12

including

THE BIG GAME
First published in Great Britain by Young Corgi Books, 1994
Text copyright © Rob Childs, 1994
Illustrations copyright © Tim Marwood, 1994

THE BIG MATCH
First published in Great Britain by Young Corgi Books, 1987
Text copyright © Rob Childs, 1987
Illustrations copyright © Tim Marwood, 1987

THE BIG PRIZE
First published in Great Britain by Young Corgi Books, 1994
Text copyright© Rob Childs, 1994
Illustrations copyright © Aidan Potts, 1994

Cover photograph taken by Oliver Hunter at Northolt
High School; with thanks to the staff and pupils of
the school for their help.
Kit in cover photograph supplied by PRO*STAR®

Young Corgi Books are published by Random House Children's Books,
61–63 Uxbridge Road, London W5 5SA,
A Random House Group Company

Addresses for companies within The Random House Group Limited
can be found at: www.randomhouse.co.uk/offices.htm

The Random House Group Limited supports The Forest Stewardship
Council (FSC), the leading international forest certification organisation.
All our titles that are printed on Greenpeace approved FSC certified paper
carry the FSC logo. Our paper procurement policy can be found at:
www.rbooks.co.uk/environment.

Printed and bound in Great Britain by
Cox & Wyman Ltd, Reading, Berkshire.

THE BIG GAME

ROB CHILDS

Illustrated by Tim Marwood

YOUNG CORGI BOOKS

*For all young footballers – keep play-ing and enjoying your soccer . . . the **BIG** game!*

www.kidsatrandomhouse.co.uk

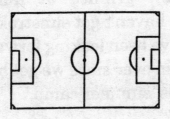

1 Summer Soccer

'Can't wait for school to start again next week.'

Christopher Weston propped himself up on his elbow in alarm. Never before had he heard his elder brother, Andrew, say that he was actually wanting to go to school.

'Are you feeling all right?' he asked, wiggling a finger in his ear as if to clear any blockage.

Andrew grinned at him. 'Don't worry, I haven't got sunstroke or anything. I've been looking forward to the new term ever since we got back from the Cubs' summer camp.'

'Why?'

'Soccer season begins of course.'

'Oh, is that all? Might have guessed.'

'What do you mean, *"is that all"?*' Andrew mocked. 'I'm going to be in the school team at last. What else is more important than that?'

Chris could have named several things, but knew it wasn't worth the effort. All Andrew had wanted to do, right through the holidays, was play football. Even today, in the middle of

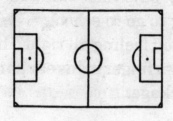

a hot afternoon, he had insisted on them having yet another kickabout in the back garden.

But now both boys were sprawled out on the lawn, stripped to the waist, taking a breather from the game in their home-made, wooden goal. They had built it themselves only days before.

'Think you stand a chance of being captain?' Chris asked instead.

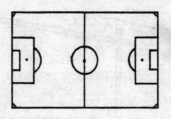

Andrew sighed and sat up. 'Nah, don't suppose so. Old Jonesy's almost bound to pick Tim Lawrence. There's only him and Duggie left from last year's team and Tim's the best player.'

'Even better than you?' Chris teased.

'Watch it! Best out of them two, I meant.'

'So why didn't the headmaster put you in the team last year too, if you're so good?' said Chris, unable to resist a further taunt, despite the risk of making Andrew mad.

'Because, little brother,' he said slowly, giving him a long, hard stare, 'me and Mr Jones don't always get on all that well. Probably thinks I'm too cheeky or something.'

Chris tried to keep a straight face, not wishing to stretch his luck too far. 'He'll need you this season, though, won't he?'

'Course he will. Got no defence, have they, without me.'

Any further boasting was stopped by a frothing mass of fur as a black-and-white collie suddenly bounded up, bent on licking his face.

'Get off, Shoot, will you!' Andrew yelled, pushing the dog away. 'I had a wash last week.'

'Here, boy,' urged Chris, patting his side. 'You can come and fan me with your tail!'

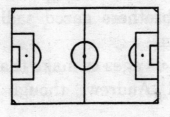

Their mother called to them from the house. 'Take Shoot for a walk, please, boys, I'm busy.'

'Aw, Mum, so are we,' Andrew grumbled. 'We're practising for the new season.'

'Doesn't look much like it to me,' she laughed. 'The dog needs some real exercise, even if you two don't.'

It was no use arguing with Mum. As she threw the lead out to them, Andrew jumped to his feet and blasted the ball at the goal in a flash of temper.

The shot smacked against the far post with a force that was more than the rickety frame could stand. The upright creaked in protest and tilted backwards, sending the crossbar crashing down to the ground.

The brothers gazed sadly at the wreckage.

'Took us ages to make that an' all,' groaned Andrew, though secretly

quite proud of the damage his power-drive had caused. 'Have to use longer nails next time.'

Chris shrugged, looking at it from a goalkeeper's point of view, his own favourite position. 'Could have been worse, I guess.'

'Oh yeah? Tell me how.'

'I might have been underneath it at the time . . .'

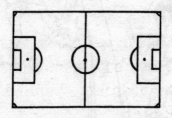

2 Hot Dog

Andrew dribbled the football along the quiet village lane towards the recreation ground, his younger brother left trailing behind with Shoot.

Several lads from Andrew's class at Danebridge Primary School, most of them two years older than Chris, were already there playing cricket.

'C'mon, you lot, put those stumps away,' he greeted them, hoofing the

17

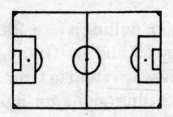

ball up into the air to make it land right in the middle of their pitch. 'It's the soccer season again now.'

John Duggan didn't need much persuading to swap sports. There was nothing he loved better than scoring goals. 'Yeah, let's have some shooting practice.'

'Good idea, our kid can go in goal for us,' Andrew said as Chris arrived.

'No way,' Simon Garner protested. 'I'm going to be school team goalie this year. I need some practice.'

'Little Westy can be behind the goal, fetching everything that big brother slices wide,' Duggie scoffed.

'I'm not just being your ball boy,'

Chris said, pulling a face. 'Besides, I'd rather go off and see Grandad.'

On his way round to Grandad's cottage, nestling right up against the recky, Chris let Shoot run free along the bank of the river Dane. He threw a few sticks for the dog to chase and twice Shoot ended up in the water, emerging to shake himself all over his young master.

Upset at first to be left out of the game, Shoot's antics soon had Chris smiling again. And his smile turned into a mischievous grin when he peered over the back garden wall of the cottage.

Grandad was asleep in an old canvas deckchair, pipe in his lap and the lawn mower standing idle on the partly-cut grass. Somehow he seemed to sense he was being watched and his eyes flickered reluctantly open.

'Sorry to disturb you, Grandad, I

can see you're busy gardening,' Chris smirked. 'Fancy a hot dog?'

'What, in this weather?' Grandad wheezed. 'You must be joking.'

'No, I'm not – here it is.'

A panting Shoot bolted through the gate to frisk around the chair, tongue lolling out of one side of his mouth.

Grandad pushed the dog playfully away as he eased himself to his feet.

'You keep them wet paws to yourself, you little pest, and that wet tongue. He's been in the river again, hasn't he?'

'Got to try and cool off somehow,' Chris said.

'Looks like you've got the right idea too, not galloping around like Andrew and the rest I can see over there.'

Chris frowned. 'They don't want me. I'm too young.'

Grandad shook his head and put his hand on the boy's bare shoulder. 'Look, it's not how old you are that matters, it's how good you are. Leave Shoot here with me for a bit and you go back and show 'em who's the real number one goalkeeper round this place!'

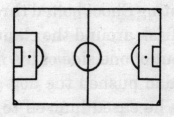

'Goal!' screamed Duggie. 'Beat you all ends up, Simon.'

'Lucky,' his friend replied. 'Had it covered till it hit a bump.'

'Our kid would have saved it,' Andrew said as Chris jogged off to fetch the ball from the undergrowth beyond the pitch.

'Come off it! If Simon couldn't, nobody could.'

'Want a bet? You wait till you see Chris in action soon for the Cubs.'

Tim Lawrence joined in. 'You two talking about the Soccer Sixes? My pack's going to win that easy.'

'Not if I can help it,' Andrew laughed. He and Tim were leading members of the two rival Cub packs in Danebridge, both hoping for success in the annual area tournament in the nearby town of Selworth.

'All my men will be in the school

team as well this year, including Duggie and Simon here,' Tim pointed out. 'Who can stop us?'

'Me and Chris for a start. We've been practising a lot in the garden. He's getting really good in goal.'

'You're a defender – your shooting would make anybody look good,' Duggie joked, making sure he kept out of Andrew's reach as he said it.

Simon booted the ball back into play to put an end to any argument and Tim laid it perfectly into Duggie's path. The striker hit it in his stride with great power, taking the keeper by surprise.

The ball flashed past him just under the crossbar, but Chris behind the goal had more time to react. He dived high to his right and clung on to the ball in mid air at full stretch in spectacular fashion.

'Well caught!' Tim cried out. 'Saved yourself a long chase.'

Chris's catch won him the chance to go in goal properly after a while, where he impressed them several times with his clean handling of the ball. Simon tried not to look too worried.

'Takes after Grandad,' Andrew said.

'What do you mean?' asked Tim.

'Grandad used to play in goal for the village team right here on this pitch. Best keeper they ever had.'

'How do you know?' Duggie sneered. 'Ever see him play?'

'Don't be stupid, course not, but loads of people have told me. He's always giving Chris tips about goal-keeping.'

'Perhaps Simon will have to watch out,' Tim smiled. 'If he starts letting in a few goals, Mr Jones might be tempted to pick your Chris instead.'

'Or even your grandad!' cackled Duggie.

Andrew retold the tale later when he and Chris collected Shoot. 'It's not just me Christopher takes after,' Grandad reminded them. 'Your dad often played in goal, too.'

The brothers looked at each other. Dad was rarely mentioned at home now, ever since he had suddenly disappeared two years ago and went to live abroad. They hadn't seen him again.

Andrew broke the awkward silence. 'Guess that goalies kind of run in our family, then, don't they?'

'Not in this heat, they don't,' Grandad chuckled. 'These days, I'm afraid, this old goalie walks!'

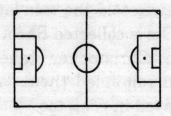

3 Six-pack

'Knew it would be you.'

The headmaster's decision to name Tim as school soccer captain came as no surprise, but Andrew still had to hide his own disappointment.

'No hard feelings, I hope,' Tim replied, realizing how much his friend had wanted the honour himself.

Andrew shook his head. 'Course not. Guess you deserve it really.'

Mr Jones had waited until halfway through the main trial game on the recky before announcing the expected news, then reshuffled the sides for the second half. Andrew and Tim now found themselves in the same team and, like everyone else, soon twigged what the headmaster was up to!

It was clear that he had put his best eleven players together to see how they shaped up. Their confidence boosted, Tim's 'A' team began to play like champions already, passing the ball around between them well and moving quickly into spaces. They all wanted it back again to show what they could do and prove that Mr Jones had made the right choice.

As for Chris, now in the 'B' team goal, he saw rather more of the ball than he might have wished. The stronger opponents swarmed around his penalty area in one attack after another, keeping him too busy to feel nervous or worry about any mistakes that he made.

He was lucky enough to get away with one fumble when an attacker somehow poked the dropped ball wide, but his next slip was more costly.

It was his own brother, too, who started the move which led to Chris's embarrassment. Andrew won the ball with a firm tackle on the halfway line, looked up and aimed a pass ahead of Tim as the captain cut in from the left touchline towards the penalty area.

Chris thought he could reach the ball first and dashed off his goal-line, but Tim was too swift for him. The young keeper was stranded out of position as the ball was whipped away from his wild lunge and stroked across to Duggie.

The unmarked striker showed no mercy. He fired his shot dead straight

through the open goal and with no net to catch it, the ball sped on and buried itself in the long grass under the trees. Chris knew the trudge to the under-growth well, but he could have done without Duggie's stinging taunt. 'Better go and ask your old grandad for some more tips, little Westy!'

Although beaten four times in the end, Chris did at least produce a few good saves too. His best moment, by far, came late in the game when he dived low to his left to smother an effort from Andrew.

'Well stopped, our kid,' Andrew praised his brother, taking his mates' teasing in good spirit. 'We'll have some more like that from you in the Sixes.'

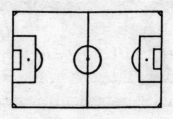

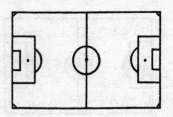

'Right!' said Akela before the start of the first group game. 'Go out and show people how you can play. Enjoy it, that's the main thing.'

The pack leader and football coach of the 1st Danebridge Cubs' team turned to Andrew, his captain. 'I'm relying on you to help the younger lads. Keep encouraging them.'

'I will, Akela,' Andrew replied, taking the job seriously. He would be leaving the Cubs soon to join the Scouts and was wanting to skipper his pack to victory in the tournament to finish on a high note.

The talents and ages of the players from the many packs in the Selworth area varied widely. Some were already

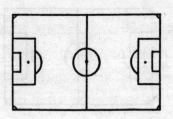

experienced footballers for their school teams, some were still too young and some, in truth, were not really good enough to be chosen yet.

But now, on a warm, sunny, September afternoon, they had their chance to take part in a big soccer tournament. They were all raring to go and do their best for the Cubs.

Andrew's team, however, got off to a bad start. Playing against a pack from Selworth itself, they were a goal down before Chris had even touched the ball.

An Asian lad, slimly built and very quick, zipped round a defender's rather nervous challenge and slid the ball past Chris from just outside the goalkeeper's semi-circular area.

'C'mon!' Andrew cried out in frustration. 'What kind of a tackle d'you call that?'

Then he caught Akela's eye and remembered his promise. 'OK, don't worry about it. That kid's so fast, just try and mark him tighter from now on, right?'

The boy nodded, feeling a little better, but he needed Andrew to come to his rescue several times more as he struggled to cope with the speed of the attacker called Rakesh. It was mostly due to the captain that there was no further scoring in the short match, but

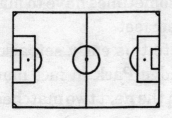

a marvellous double save from Chris near the end prevented a heavier defeat.

First he parried an awkward skidding drive and then, as the ball rebounded outside the area, it was Rakesh who pounced on it before anyone else. He could hardly believe it when the goalkeeper recovered in time to block his shot as well and scoop the ball over the crossbar.

'How did you keep that one out?' Rakesh grinned, entering the area to help him up. 'Dead cert second goal that was.'

'Just hit my legs,' Chris admitted modestly. But as Grandad had often told him, he knew that even the best goalies sometimes have to make saves with their feet.

Despite this early setback, the 1st Danebridge Pack in fact managed to win both the next two matches against

weaker sides and qualify for the quarter-finals as runners-up in their group.

Mr Jones arrived on the scene at this stage in the hope of watching many of his own soccer squad in action, just in time to see Chris play a blinder.

'Promising young keeper, your grandson,' he said to Grandad after a fierce volley was pushed to safety round a post.

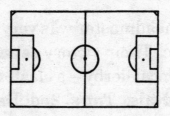

Grandad had helped to transport the Cubs to the tournament, ready as always to support Andrew and Chris in their sporting activities in any way that he could. 'Aye, that's true,' he nodded proudly. 'You haven't got a better goalie in your school from what I've seen.'

Mr Jones smiled. 'His chance will come one day, that's for sure.'

Chris helped that future day come a little closer with a whole series of excellent saves, keeping a clean sheet for the first time in the competition. And to complete a fine family double act, Andrew scored the only goal of the game, his third altogether, which put them through to the semi-finals.

The headmaster was very glad that
he came. Their victory set up a fasci-
nating local derby – a clash with their
great rivals, Tim's 2nd Danebridge
Pack!

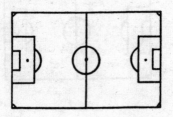

4 Do Your Best

'Good luck, everyone,' Akela called out to both the Danebridge packs before the kick-off. 'May the best team win.'

'Yeah – as long as it's us,' Andrew added under his breath, certain that Tim would be thinking exactly the same thing.

Beating their friends would in many ways be more important than winning the actual tournament itself.

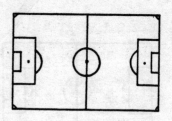

Each pack's pride was at stake. All the pre-match joking and mickey-taking between the players would be nothing, they feared, compared to what the losers might have to suffer afterwards from their cocky conquerors.

Most of Duggie's jibes were aimed at Chris in an attempt to put him off. 'Well, look who it is – our little ball boy again!'

Chris flushed, but tried to give back as good as he got. 'This time I'll be saving your shots in front of the goal, not behind it.'

Duggie wasted no time in testing him out, too, when the game began. He hit a shot from the wing which slithered along the ground, bang on target, but the goalkeeper was equal to it.

He made sure his body was right behind his hands, as Grandad always insisted when they practised together, and it was a good job that he did so. The ball bobbled through his grasp but thudded against his chest, and he was able to dive on to it again before it escaped from the area.

At the other end, Simon proved just as safe and the two goalies kept the scoresheet blank at half-time. Straight after the change-round, however, Andrew, of all people, missed a clear chance to put his team ahead.

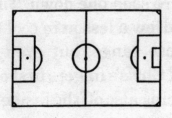

With only Simon to beat, he blazed the ball wildly over the bar when a careful, accurate side-footer was all that was needed to score.

Sadly, instead of being a goal up, they were soon one down. Tim was to give Andrew a lesson in cool finishing from close range, but even his shot brushed Chris's fingers first on its way in, glancing also off the inside of a post.

Andrew decided to stay up in attack now to try and snatch an equalizer, but it was a gamble that didn't pay off. His absence from defence left a large hole which Duggie soon used to his own benefit.

Receiving a pass from Tim, he found himself in so much space, he had time to give the young goalkeeper a triumphant grin before hammering the ball past him. Chris's only consolation was that at least there was a net this time to save him another long trek.

At the final whistle, Andrew was big enough to go up and shake Tim's hand and wish him luck, but the 2-0 defeat hurt him badly.

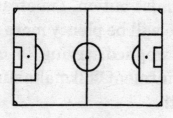

'Never mind, Andrew, you can't win 'em all,' Grandad said as the brothers joined him on the touchline to watch the Final. 'This is one big game you'll have to miss out on, I'm afraid.'

'There will be plenty more to come,' Andrew replied, trying to cover his disappointment. 'I'll make sure of that all right!'

Tim's 2nd Danebridge Cubs' Pack believed that the Cup was as good as in the trophy cabinet in their village hut. Nothing could stand in their way now – apart from the 9th Selworth outfit and Rakesh.

It was the winger's pace which took them by surprise, just as it had Andrew's side earlier in the tournament. Rakesh was allowed to run free down the right touchline and his cross was tucked neatly past Simon into the corner of the goal by the Selworth captain.

'Perhaps we should have warned them about that lad,' Akela smiled.

'He sure needs special marking,' said Andrew. 'Give him too much room

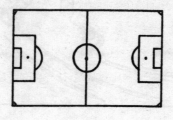

and he'll take any defence apart.'

As if to prove his words, Rakesh sped clear again but his shot on the run clipped the woodwork. It was the only piece of luck that Tim's team enjoyed. For once, Duggie seemed to have completely lost his magic touch and chance after chance at the other end went begging.

Usually the deadliest of strikers, he sliced one shot so far wide, the ball hit the corner flag instead of the goal, and then poked another tame effort straight at the keeper. Not even the captain could find his true form and inspire his pack to victory, missing an open goal himself.

They ended up losing 1-0 and both Tim and Andrew had to look on enviously as the Selworth captain lifted the Sixes Cup to great cheers.

'If we could have fielded a joint

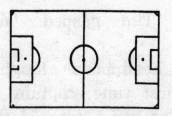

Danebridge team, they wouldn't have beaten us, I know,' sighed Tim.

'Yeah, that's right,' Andrew agreed. 'Six or eleven-a-side, they'd have no chance against us at full strength.'

'We'd slaughter 'em!' put in Duggie.

Mr Jones had come up behind them unnoticed. 'Well played, boys,' he began, making them jump, and they whirled round to face him. 'Glad to hear you'd all love another crack at them. It so happens I've just fixed up our first league match – and guess who we've got?'

They followed his eyes towards the grinning group of Selworth boys, holding up their medals for the photographs in the sunshine.

'No!' Tim gasped. 'You don't mean . . .'

The headmaster laughed. 'Yes, right first time, captain. Selworth School at home, ten o'clock kick-off next Saturday morning!'

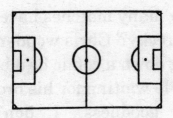

5 Debut Day

'You will be watching, won't you, Grandad?'

Andrew had dashed straight to the cottage after the final practice session for the Selworth game, almost bursting with excitement. He had been picked to play at centre-back, right at the heart of the defence.

'Course I will,' Grandad reassured him. 'I'll be here, as always, leaning on my old garden wall – my own little grandstand view.'

'How many matches have you seen on the recky?' Chris wondered aloud, putting down a comic he'd been reading while waiting for his brother.

'Oh, goodness, I don't know,' Grandad laughed. 'Hundreds and hundreds, must be, and thousands of players – good and bad.'

'Anybody famous?' Andrew asked keenly.

Grandad smoothed down his moustache in thought, his eyes twinkling. 'Well, not as a footballer, as far as I can recall. Mind you, we did have a bank robber once! Got arrested after scoring a hat-trick . . .'

'You're making that up,' Andrew cried. 'C'mon, Grandad, I'm being serious. If nobody from our village has ever become a professional footballer, my ambition is to be the first!'

'Well, every future soccer star's got to start their career somewhere,' Grandad said, sensing the boy's determination. 'And I guess Danebridge recky is as good a place as any.'

Chris butted in again. 'I just want to play in goal for Danebridge like you did, Grandad – and Dad, as well, of course.'

Grandad was delighted. 'And I've

still got an ambition left, too, y'know – even at my age.'

'What's that?' they chorused.

'Well, now that you're both getting old enough, I'm looking forward to seeing the two of you play together here for the school team.'

Chris gave a little groan. 'Sorry, Grandad, you might have to wait a while yet. By the time I get chosen, Andrew will have left.'

The old man smiled and nudged Chris gently on the arm with his elbow. 'Doubt it. From what I've seen, reckon you'll be wearing that goalkeeper's green jersey sooner than you think.'

Andrew tried to steer the talk back on to his own debut, never mind his kid brother's. 'We're after revenge on Saturday – now it's a proper eleven-a-side match, we're going to show 'em who's boss.'

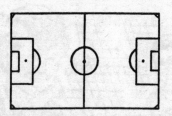

'Maybe, but just don't go building up your hopes too much,' Grandad said wisely, starting to light his curved pipe. 'It's a funny old game, football. And I should know, I've seen it all — anything can happen . . .'

'That Rakesh is only one of their subs,' Andrew gasped, spotting the Asian lad still in his tracksuit top among Selworth's light-blue kit.

Simon broke off from their pre-match practice to stand and stare. 'You're right. Good news, that is, I'd been dreading facing him again.'

'Bad news, I'd say,' Andrew reck-oned. 'They must be better than we

thought, if they can afford to leave out someone like him.'

The defender rolled up the sleeves of his red and white striped shirt, so thrilled to be wearing the Danebridge colours for the first time. 'Anyway, I don't care who's playing, I'm ready for 'em,' he stated boldly. 'Let's get kicked off.'

As the Danebridge and Selworth

teams lined up on a bright, autumn morning, Chris was already in action, keeping goal between two sports bags in a kickabout game with several friends near the main pitch. As he swooped on to a low shot before it could sneak through, he recognized a voice behind him.

'Can I join in? I get fed up just hanging around, watching.'

Chris stood up, still holding on to

the ball. 'I remember you from the Cubs' Sixes,' he said shyly.

'I haven't forgotten you either,' Rakesh replied. 'You stopped us scoring a few more goals with saves like that.'

'You were brill,' Chris said, returning the compliment. 'Why aren't you playing today?'

'Only got picked as sub,' he explained with a shrug. 'The others are all a year older than me.'

'I know how you feel,' Chris sighed. 'Even my big brother's had to wait till now to make his debut for the school.'

Rakesh grinned as Andrew was pointed out. 'Oh, it's him, is it? I've still got the bruises to show for his tackling last week! Tried to slow me down a bit.'

Chris laughed. 'Well he didn't succeed.'

'No, and I hope to prove that to him myself later. Teacher's said I'll be on

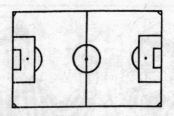

after half-time so I want to be nicely warmed up by then.'

Their game re-started with Rakesh but before he'd even had a kick, a cheer went up and they all glanced round. Too late! The Danebridge players were already celebrating Duggie's first goal of the season.

The younger lads missed seeing his second as well. But by that time, Rakesh had also scored two of his own, making Chris regret his daft decision to let him play for the other side in their kickabout game.

The Selworth keeper was none too happy either. He had been at fault with the opening goal and just when he'd thought the striker's next shot

was going way over the bar, the ball
dipped down late and flew in just
beneath the high crossbar. Duggie
knew the size of the big goals on the
recky pitch far better than he did.

'Fantastic!' whooped Andrew after
he'd raced up and slapped Duggie's
raised hand in delight. 'Maybe this is
going to be dead easy after all.'

'Long way to go yet,' Tim warned

him. 'You just make sure they don't score any.'

As Andrew took up his position again in defence, he realized somebody else was also trying to tell him to calm down. The signals from the garden wall served to remind him of one of Grandad's favourite sayings.

'A game's never won until the referee blows the final whistle.'

And before this match was over, all the players were going to learn that important soccer lesson . . .

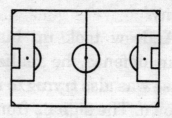

6 Great Game

Andrew was furious. With himself and with the other defenders.

'C'mon, that was a sloppy goal to give away,' he yelled as Simon miserably fished the ball out the back of the net.

Nor was their captain best pleased with his team's poor marking at a corner, allowing the Selworth player far too much freedom to control the ball and shoot.

'Told you all to watch out,' Tim said crossly. 'Now we've gone and let them back in the game.'

As Tim feared, the goal perked the visitors up and they were on top for the rest of the first half. Andrew worked like a beaver to prevent the defensive dam bursting under the pressure of a flood of attacks and pulled off an amazing escape act just before the interval.

The equalizer looked certain when Simon was caught out of his goal and the ball was lobbed over his head. Everyone, it seemed, stopped and gave up to watch it bouncing towards the welcoming net – but not Andrew.

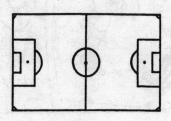

Hoping against hope, he simply kept chasing, desperate to reach the ball before it crossed the line. And he did – just! With less than a metre to spare, Andrew somehow managed to hook the ball away, tumbling head over heels into the goal himself instead.

He was so tangled up in the netting, trapped by his studs like a helpless fly in a giant spider's web, that play had to be halted while the referee went to his rescue. Andrew emerged red-faced, but grinning, to loud applause from the spectators.

'You're a better goal-hanger than me,' Duggie joked as they gathered round Mr Jones for the half-time pep talk.

Chris joined them, his own game now abandoned. 'What were you doing dangling upside-down in the goal?' he asked when the group broke up.

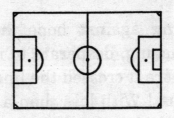

Andrew was stunned, unable to believe that his brother had missed his best moment. 'What a stupid question! You mean you didn't see my brilliant clearance off the line?'

Chris shook his head. 'Sorry. When I looked round to check what the cheering was about, all I could see was you doing a headstand.'

Andrew felt like hitting him. 'Typical! Sunbathing, were you?'

'I was playing football with Rakesh actually,' Chris defended himself. 'He's on great form – we just couldn't stop him scoring.'

'I'll deal with him all right,' Andrew boasted. 'You watch.'

'Oh, I will,' Chris said cheekily. 'I'm not going to miss this!'

Even Grandad had come for a closer look at the second half, appearing on the touchline with Shoot lying at his side. 'Well played,' he called to Andrew. 'Keep it up, don't relax.'

There was no chance for anybody to do that, especially with Rakesh now sent on, as promised, to bomb down the right wing. The left back couldn't match such explosive pace and Andrew had to cover across twice in the first few minutes to help him out.

But not even Andrew could stop the winger for long from levelling the

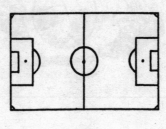

69

scores. Rakesh outsprinted everybody to race clear for goal and then fooled Simon with a last-second body swerve, dribbling the ball past him before tapping it into the empty goal.

Andrew stood dejected, hands on hips, shaking his head at how they had thrown away a two-goal lead. He glared at Rakesh's little dance of celebration. 'Well you won't be doing that again,' he said under his breath. 'Not if I can do anything about it.'

Five minutes later, Andrew was as good as his word, but not quite in the way that he'd intended. Seeing Rakesh this time cut inside from the wing, hurtling for goal with the ball under the close control of his flying feet, Andrew homed in across his path like a torpedo.

Rakesh sensed the danger and increased his speed even more, the extra burst taking him into the penalty area. Just as he steadied himself a fraction for the shot, however, the defender struck. Andrew stretched out a long leg to nudge the ball away – but didn't quite make it. His boot caught Rakesh instead, knocking him off-balance and sending him sprawling to the ground.

'Penalty!'

Andrew, down on his knees, held up his hands in horror and then clamped them to his ears as if to deafen the appeals.

And to make matters worse, as the referee pointed to the penalty spot, there was a pitch invasion. Two boys tried to stop the intruder, but the first Andrew knew about it was when his face was licked.

Shoot had been startled by the sudden loud shouts and leapt up, jerking the lead from Grandad's loose grip. Seeing Andrew nearby, he ran to him

in greeting, barking with excitement, but soon realized his master was in no mood to play. His tail disappeared between his legs.

'Get him off!' Andrew snarled as Chris came on to grab the trailing lead. 'Suppose you saw what happened that time OK, didn't you?'

"Fraid so, but don't get mad at Shoot,' Chris said, tugging the dog

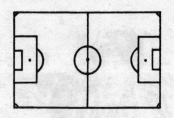

away. 'He might be the only friend you've got if this penalty costs us the match!'

Andrew stood on the edge of the area with all the other players to watch the duel between goalkeeper and penalty-taker, praying that Simon might yet save him. As the Selworth captain made contact, Simon dived to his right, but the ball flew dead straight. If the keeper had stayed where he was, it would have hit him smack in the stomach.

'Forget about it, Andrew,' Grandad called out as Danebridge now found themselves 2-3 down. 'Just get on with the game.'

'Your grandad's right,' added Tim.

'Can't be helped, you did your best. About the only other one round here who could have caught up with Rakesh like that was your dog.'

'Yeah, and I bet he would have tripped him up too!' grunted Duggie.

Andrew tried to look on the bright side again. 'C'mon, team, we can still do it,' he shouted to urge them all on. 'There's still time.'

But when he saw the referee carefully studying his watch, Andrew knew there could not really be much longer left. Determined to make up for his mistake, he went into the next tackle on Rakesh just as strongly as ever and this time won the ball cleanly. Moving it on to Tim, Andrew kept charging forward, adding his own weight to the attack as well.

The powerful defender strode deep into the Selworth half, demanding the ball back again. When it came,

Andrew hit it first time, hard and low towards goal, but he was out of luck. An opponent managed to get his body in the way and deflect the shot wide.

Andrew decided to stay up for the left-wing corner, hoping for a possible header at goal himself. Both he and Duggie lurked by the far post as Tim curled the ball high and long towards them with the inside of his right boot – but neither of Tim's intended targets could reach it.

Nor could the goalkeeper. The ball swung over everybody's heads and swirled into the top corner of the net, untouched.

'Fluke!' yelled Duggie into Tim's ear as the captain was half-suffocated under the crush of his jubilant team-mates.

'Who cares?' Tim choked back. 'They all count.'

To the relief of two exhausted sides,

the referee blew soon afterwards for full-time with the match tied at three goals each.

Mr Jones passed Grandad on his way to the changing hut. 'Phew! What a game to start the season!' the headmaster exclaimed. 'Your Andrew certainly had his ups and downs, but I reckon he was just about *"Man of the Match"* in the end.'

'Aye, but don't tell him,' Grandad laughed, 'or we'll never hear the last of it!'

Andrew trotted over and bent down to make friends again with Shoot.

'Don't worry, Shoot's forgiven you already,' Chris smiled. 'He doesn't care what the score was!'

'The dog's got more sense,' said Grandad. 'It's how you play that's important, not the final result. Football's only a game after all.'

'But it's a great game,' Andrew enthused. 'The best in the world!'

Grandad chuckled. 'Even if you lose?'

Andrew hesitated only for a moment. 'Win or lose,' he said firmly.

'Or draw,' added Chris, giving Shoot an extra little pat.

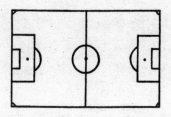

THE END

The Big Match

Rob Childs
Illustrated by Tim Marwood

YOUNG CORGI BOOKS

For my own Grandad, and those like him,
with thanks for all their sporting
encouragement to youngsters.

1 Lost Ball

'Great save, Chris!' shouted Andrew as his younger brother pushed yet another of his best shots round the post. 'You're unbeatable today.'

That was praise indeed from someone who played in the school football team.

Christopher Weston grinned and lay stretched out on the back garden lawn, posing for imaginary sports photographers. He wanted nothing more than to be in the Danebridge

Primary School team like Andrew was. He dreamed about it almost every night — and day-dreamed in class too, if his teacher let him.

He kept telling himself that his own chance to play would come soon. But really he knew he was going to have to wait, somehow, until he was a bit older.

Not that he wanted to be just an ordinary defender like his brother. No! Chris's single aim in life was to wear the special green goalkeeper's jersey with the large black number 1 stitched on the back.

Suddenly he jolted up. Andrew had quickly fetched the ball and was juggling it in the air, setting himself up for the shot as it fell.

He was already screaming,

'GOAL!' as Chris leapt and punched it high over the crossbar. The excited cries died in dismay as they watched the ball clip the top of the fence and flop out of sight into the neighbouring garden.

'Oh, no! That does it,' Andrew groaned, glaring. 'Now look what you've gone and done.'

'It wasn't my fault. Why blame me?' Chris complained in return. 'It's

11

usually you who blasts it next door.'

Andrew went into a sulk. 'That was heading straight for the top corner. A goal all the way.'

'Until I fisted it!' Chris added, cheekily.

His brother sighed. 'Why do you have to be so good in goal?'

It was said in frustration, but he could not have paid Chris a better compliment. He loved keeping goal and wasn't interested in playing in any other position. Their grandad always said that he was a born goalie, and Chris was determined to prove him right.

Andrew continued to grumble.

'I bet it's landed right in the middle of the witch's flower-bed. She'll never let us have it back again.'

The 'witch' in question was old Mrs Witchell. She lived by herself now, a frail, wrinkled lady with a quick temper and rarely a good word for noisy young boys. They were generally careful not to cross her — especially near Hallowe'en time.

'She'll be hopping mad,' he went on, gloomily. 'Remember, she threatened last time to have our football banned in the garden if it happened again.'

'She can't do that!' Chris gasped, horrified. 'Can she?'

They gazed with renewed pride at the small wooden goal they had clumsily nailed together during the summer; in their eyes it would have graced Wembley Stadium itself.

'We've got to do something,' declared Andrew in desperation.

'Like what? Please, dear little, old witchy, please may we have our ball back?' Chris mocked.

'Don't be stupid. No, we'll just have to sneak in and grab it before she notices.'

'Oh, yeah! Just like that. She might be lying in wait . . . and put a spell on us!'

Chris could already feel his heart-beat increasing at the mere thought of all the risks involved.

'Pooh! You are a baby sometimes, little brother Christopher. You're chicken!'

'No, I'm not.' He hated being called by his full name and knew it was only used to taunt him at times like this.

'Okay, let's go then,' Andrew challenged, and pushed him towards the gate before he could resist. He would never have admitted it to Chris, of course, but he didn't fancy raiding the witch's garden all by himself.

'Hold on, hold on!' Chris managed to blurt out. 'We can't just walk straight in there.'

'No, you're right,' Andrew considered. 'We must have a plan. This is going to need split-second timing . . .'

So it was that, five minutes later, Chris found himself timidly tapping at Mrs Witchell's green front door.

His part in their tactics, as far as he understood, was to create a diversion while Andrew sneaked round the back to get the ball. Right now, however, his older and wiser brother was crouching low behind the hedge, waiting for the moment either to advance or retreat.

At last the door slowly creaked open and the old woman's crinkly face creased up even more as she frowned when she saw who had disturbed her afternoon nap.

'Hmm . . . yes?' she demanded icily. 'What is it, boy? Speak up.'

For several seconds Chris lost his nerve and also his tongue, but then garbled out their story about collecting for the school jumble sale. He began to lose what little faith he had in the plan as he heard the words tumble out of his mouth, and he tailed off lamely, ' . . . er . . . anything would do . . . '

He started to back away under Mrs Witchell's hard, suspicious stare. She appeared to be about to shoo him off when her expression suddenly changed.

'Hmm ... wait a minute, not so fast. There is something. I've been meaning to get rid of them for ages. Stay where you are while I go and fetch them. Don't move.'

Chris was by now so terrified, he didn't think he could move his feet anyway.

She closed the door and immediately Andrew raced up the short path past him, ducking under the side window on his way to the back garden.

His luck was in. There was the white plastic ball nestling beneath a small shrub on the flower border. He just had to pray that she would be too busy searching to glance out of the window and spot him.

Holding his breath, he slipped along the edge of the neatly-mown lawn and stepped carefully between the plants. 'Good,' he thought, 'no damage done.'

He grabbed his prize and clutched it tightly to his chest, then turned and fled back, throwing caution now to the wind. His heart was pounding the blood deafeningly into his ears in fear and excitement as he saw Chris frantically signalling that the coast was still clear.

Without checking, he ran full tilt past the house and didn't stop until he reached the safety of their own garden. He collapsed into the goalmouth, hugging himself and the ball with equal delight.

Chris felt awfully tempted to follow him, but somehow steeled himself to stay and see it through to the end. There was, in fact, to be a jumble sale shortly, so he decided he might as well get something for it after all his trouble.

But their plan had only just succeeded. No sooner had Andrew scampered out of sight when Mrs Witchell loomed over Chris again.

'What's the matter with you, boy? You look scared to death.'

'Nothing, Mrs Witch — ell.'

He almost forgot to add on the ending to her name.

'Hmm . . . ' she murmured again through closed lips. 'Well, here you are. Have these, and don't come back

pestering me for more.'

Chris stammered some thanks and gratefully hurried out of her clutches, arriving back almost trembling with relief.

'We did it! We did it!' whooped Andrew. 'We tricked the old witch and got away with it.'

'We also got these.' Chris held out a pair of frayed, brown gloves for inspection. 'Just right for the jumble.'

They laughed and re-lived their daring raid. Chris even tried the gloves on in an act of bravado.

'Hey! They fit me as well.'

'C'mon, stop messing about now. Take them off and get back in goal.'

Andrew was still so pleased with himself that he took a huge swing at the ball for his first shot and its speed and power took Chris completely by surprise. He didn't even make a move for it. He could only watch it smack against the top of the bar and loop up high into the air at a crazy angle.

In horror and disbelief, they saw it sail right over the fence and disappear into that same forbidden garden again.

'Oh no!' they chorused, and both sank to their knees to listen for any sound.

Silence.

'Er . . . I suppose we could try it again,' suggested Andrew, with a sheepish grin.

Chris exploded. 'No chance! You have got to be joking! I'm not going through all that a second time for anything.'

That was one ball, sadly, they never did see again.

2 Great News

'Christopher Weston!'

The sudden announcement of his own name startled him out of a daydream.

'Stay behind after this assembly to see me,' continued Mr Jones, the headmaster of Danebridge Primary School, before moving on to appeal for more jumble to be brought in for the sale.

Chris felt himself going bright red as many eyes burned into him. To avoid them, he turned his head round to pick out Andrew who was sitting several rows behind him among the top juniors. All he received was an unsympathetic shrug of the shoulders.

He sighed. More trouble, no doubt, but he couldn't think what or why. Then his blood ran cold.

The old witch!

He supposed she must have discovered their trick and complained — and she hadn't seen Andrew, of course. Chris groaned to himself. He would probably be accused of stealing the stupid gloves or something. He had forgotten to bring them into school so there was not even any proof of his good intentions.

The others rose to leave the hall and

he braced himself. Whatever happened, he decided, he would not tell tales on Andrew. But even so, he wished they were walking into Mr Jones's office together.

'Close the door, Christopher, please.'

Before the headmaster could say anything else, Chris blurted out. 'I'm sorry, Mr Jones.'

He looked surprised. 'Sorry? What about?'

Chris hesitated, a little in doubt.

'For whatever I've done.'

Mr Jones laughed out loud, so much so that even Chris realized he must have misread the situation.

'You seem to have a guilty conscience about something, my boy, but we won't go into that just now.

I'm not telling you off, don't worry. Quite the opposite, in fact.'

He paused to make sure he had the boy's full attention.

'I've got some excellent news for you. Something I know you've been longing to hear.'

Chris was now even more puzzled than before.

'I found out yesterday that Simon Garner is ill and will not be able to play on Saturday.'

Mr Jones was deliberately spooning out the news in small, tantalizing helpings to enjoy the effect it was having upon his young pupil. Chris's eyes were opening wide with the dawn of understanding.

Simon was the regular school team goalkeeper.

He could hardly wait for the next magic words as all fears of the witch were blown out of his mind.

'Well, I've thought very hard about it,' the headmaster smiled, 'and I've decided to pick you for your first match in goal for us.'

Chris tried to say something, but his throat tightened and he remained speechless.

'Congratulations! You're a very promising goalie, and I know you won't let us down.'

29

Chris was in too much of a shock to grasp anything else that was said, and he drifted back along the corridor to his classroom on a cloud.

'You're making it up!' Andrew exclaimed at morning break. 'He wouldn't risk picking a second year for a vital Cup game. We're playing Shenby School, our main rivals.'

Chris was a little hurt by his brother's outburst. Part of the thrill for him was being chosen to play in the same side as Andrew. He had not stopped to think that Andrew might view his unexpected selection in rather a different light.

Like most boys, Andrew had had to wait until his final year at the school before being considered good enough for a place in the team, and he now enjoyed the respect and sense of importance it gave him. The sudden news that his kid brother was pinching some of the glory was a bit hard to swallow all at once.

To his credit, however, he tried hard to hide his feelings and was big enough to accept the new situation and come to terms with it by the time the bell went. 'Don't worry,' he told Chris as they lined up. 'Us defenders will look after you. Shenby will have to get past me first to reach you.'

One person who would be sure to welcome his great news, Chris knew, was their grandad who was always their biggest football fan.

That evening, as usual, Grandad was leaning over the back garden wall of his stone cottage that looked across the village recreation ground, puffing contentedly on his curved pipe. Chris ran up to him, his face flushed with excitement.

'Well, what an honour!' Grandad

said proudly. 'What did I tell you?'

He nudged Chris gently on the arm with his elbow as he often did when giving a piece of good advice or encouragement. 'I said you'd be in the team before you reckoned. To me, you're better than that Simon already.'

Chris grinned sheepishly at such praise. 'I don't know, Grandad. Simon's a good keeper. He'll be back when he's well again, I expect. It's just for this one match.'

'You never know. This is your big chance. Take it, and show them how good you are. Mr Jones has thrown you in at the deep end to see whether you sink or swim.'

He used his pipe this time to give Chris an affectionate prod to stress his point. 'I reckon you'll swim all right.'

They looked over to where Andrew and some of his friends were kicking a ball about on the village team's pitch. The primary school had to use it too, as their own playing field was too small for proper matches.

Chris was comforted by the thought that Grandad would be here, close by, to boost his confidence on Saturday. He always watched his games lessons too and usually made helpful comments afterwards about his performance in goal.

'Try to learn from your mistakes,' was one of Grandad's favourite sayings. 'It might stop you giving away a similar goal in future.'

They chatted for a while longer

until Grandad said, 'You ought to go across and join in. It looks like they need a decent keeper and you need some extra practice. You're in training for the big match now, you know.'

He gave his grandson a wink to send him on his way and then smiled. He felt sure he was looking forward to Saturday almost as much as the lad himself!

3 In Training

'C'mon! Simon gobbles them up for breakfast,' came the stinging criticism as Chris fumbled a shot early in their kick-about. 'We'd better not get knocked out of the Cup because of you, or you've had it!'

The threat was made by Simon's best mate, John Duggan, too low for Andrew to hear, but forcibly enough to leave Chris in no doubt who would be blamed for any defeat, whether his fault or not.

He quickly realized that he could not win their respect merely because he was Andrew's brother. Two years or so difference in age was a wide gap to bridge, unless he could prove himself in their company. He knew he would have to earn recognition of his goalkeeping ability by his own efforts.

Soon afterwards Duggan was put clean through to goal from a brilliant pass by school team captain Tim Lawrence, and Chris immediately went out towards him to try and narrow the shooting angle.

The two of them were on collision course and Duggan drove in extra hard as Chris dived bravely down at his feet, catching him a painful blow on the shoulder with his right boot. Chris still managed to cling on to the ball, though, and struggled to his feet, rubbing the spot rather gingerly.

Andrew squared up angrily to John Duggan. 'That was a deliberate dirty foul!'

'Rubbish!' Duggan snarled back. 'He's got to toughen up and expect a few knocks if he wants to be a goalie.'

Andrew was fired up enough to want to take their argument further, but Tim stepped between them just in time to cool rising tempers.

'Go easy, Duggie, we don't want another keeper crocked.'

The forward turned away. 'Huh! It wouldn't matter. Somebody else could go in goal . . . somebody *older*.'

'There's nobody else better than our Chris,' Andrew blurted out. But then he checked himself, surprised at the strength of his support for his younger brother against one of his own group of friends. He was the only one allowed to insult Chris and get away with it!

'It's okay, Andrew,' Chris put in. 'Thanks for sticking up for me, but let's just get on with the football. I'm all right.'

There were a few more lingering glares, but the incident was put behind them in the general hurly-

burly of the game, which continued until the light began to fade.

'Let's pack up now — it's getting too dark,' Tim decided. 'Remember we've got our main practice here tomorrow after school.'

He went up to Chris. 'Well played. You made some good stops. You'll do for me.'

Chris was delighted to find the captain on his side and forgot about

42

the ache in his shoulder until their grandad asked about it before they went home.

'It's fine. Just a bit sore, that's all.'

Grandad nodded his approval. 'Good. You'll certainly get far worse cracks than that playing in goal. You know what the old saying is, don't you?'

'What's that?' Chris grinned, already guessing the reply.

'All goalkeepers are crazy! That's what they always say,' he chuckled, and knocked his pipe on the stone wall to empty out its charred remains.

The following afternoon the school soccer squad clattered across the footbridge over the river Dane, which wrapped itself around the recreation

ground on its rippling way through the village.

Mr Jones brought up the rear of the party and quickly organized the boys into small groups to practise their passing and ball control skills. He then took the new young keeper into the goalmouth with two others to help in order to give him some special individual attention.

Soon Chris was diving about in all directions as they kicked and threw balls at him at different speeds and heights. Some bounced awkwardly just in front of him while others had him stretching upwards to reach. All the time the headmaster encouraged him either to hold on to the ball or to push it right away to one side out of danger.

'Try to get some part of your body
behind your hands if you can,' he told
him. 'There's nothing worse than letting a ball slip through your fingers
and then between your legs as well for
a goal.'

He knew, though, that Chris had
quite a safe pair of hands and usually
positioned himself well to deal with
most shots. Even so, when the ball
was hit well above his mop of fair hair

he had little chance of stopping it in these goals, which were really too high and wide for boys of this age.

Taking a brief break from the coaching, Mr Jones exchanged a few words over the wall with the boy's grandad who was watching with great interest. 'Still got a lot to learn of course, young Chris, but he's coming on well. He's so keen.'

'Aye, he is that,' the old man

replied proudly. 'He'll make a fine keeper one day, you mark my words.'

The session included a vigorous seven-a-side game with everyone trying extra hard to impress in the hope of getting picked for the Cup match. Chris, in fact, did not have the happiest of times in this, and blamed himself for a couple of goals he let in, especially one by John Duggan.

He allowed the big lad's powerful challenge to distract him enough to take his eye off the ball for a vital second. He dropped it at Duggan's feet, allowing him to poke it over the unguarded line.

'Got you rattled, have I?' he jeered. 'That's no good. If Shenby find out you're a softie, they'll murder you!'

Chris ignored the unfair jibe and renewed his concentration on the

49

game, but he guessed Andrew had overheard. In the next attack the defender took revenge by crunching into Duggan — hard but cleanly — to win the ball just as he was about to try another shot.

Finally the headmaster gathered them together to give out further bits of advice and then announce the team.

'It should be a good close match,' he predicted before sending them

home, 'but win or lose, I hope you all enjoy it. It's the way you play that matters, remember, not the final result.'

The two brothers trailed off for their tea still full of talk about the coming game. The prospect of their playing together for the first time was now beginning to appeal to Andrew more and more. 'Duggie's okay, really,' he tried to explain. 'Once you get to know him. It's just that he hates to lose at anything, despite what old Jonesy always says.'

'Well, he's not exactly helping our chances by getting at me all the time,' Chris grumbled.

'Oh, forget it. He's like that with everyone. He's seen you make enough good saves to know you'll be all right.'

'That's the trouble. I hope I will. I'm getting scared about perhaps letting in a daft goal that costs us the match.'

Andrew laughed. 'You won't do anything like that. You'll play a blinder on Saturday. I mean, with you in goal and me in defence, Shenby don't stand a chance of scoring!'

Chris only wished it would be as easy as Andrew made it sound. But as it turned out, Andrew too had cause to regret his choice of words.

During the next two days at school Chris had little time for brooding about what might happen, as his class teacher worked him extra hard to prevent his thoughts from wandering too much on to football. But Chris didn't really mind. It was all worth it. He was soon going to wear that treasured green jersey.

At breaks he could hardly stay away from the sports notice-board. His eyes were drawn to the list of names for the Shenby match. It gave him a delicious tingle up and down his spine every time he saw written beside the goalkeeping position the

name . . . C. Weston.

He had to keep checking that it was still there. It was somehow proof that he had made it at last. Nothing could stop him from playing now. Nothing!

Except perhaps for a dramatic, unfortunate change in the weather . . .

4 *Kick-Off*

'Is it never going to stop?' Chris whined.

The two boys stared miserably out of their rain-spattered bedroom window.

'It's been raining for hours,' Andrew muttered. 'The match will be called off at this rate.'

Chris was appalled.

'Off! You mean, cancelled?'

His dreams began to disappear down the drain with all the rainwater.

'Could be. Pitch waterlogged, they call it.'

'It can't be!' Chris cried out. 'Simon'll be fit again then before I even get a chance to play.'

They looked at each other with equal dismay.

'C'mon, it'll probably be okay,' said Andrew more optimistically. 'No use worrying about it. Let's try and get some sleep.'

They lay in the darkened room, Chris too tense and nervous to close his eyes as he thought about Andrew's final words before he had switched off the light. 'If we do play tomorrow, it's sure going to be muddy. We'll be sliding about all over the place. Great!'

But the likelihood of a slippery ball

to handle was not helping Chris's peace of mind at all.

Suddenly he sat bolt upright in bed.

'Gloves!' he exclaimed loudly. 'Oh no! My goalie's gloves. I've left them at school.'

'You idiot!' came a weary reply from nearby. 'You're hopeless.'

'What can I do?'

'Nothing. They won't go and open up the school just for you, so you'll just have to manage without. Serves you right — it might improve your memory in future.'

Slowly, however, even the sleepy Andrew began to appreciate the possible serious consequences for the team. 'Haven't you got any others to wear?'

Chris shook his head. 'Only my

ordinary gloves. Mum would go mad if I messed them up.'

They considered the problem for several minutes until Chris let out a whoop.

'The witch's gloves!'

He scrambled out of bed and fished them out from the top drawer of his cabinet.

'I thought you'd already taken them into school for the jumble,' Andrew said.

'I kept forgetting,' Chris confessed, and then laughed. 'You see, it helps to have a bad memory sometimes!'

Andrew gave up and watched his brother pull them on.

'They're nice and rough so I'll be able to grip the ball okay, I reckon. Good old witchy! Hey! They might even have a lucky magic spell on them.'

'Fat chance of that,' Andrew scoffed. 'More likely to be unlucky, if you ask me. But I suppose they're better than nothing. How do they feel?'

'Ace! They fit like a glove!' Chris joked.

Andrew collapsed back on to his pillow with a groan and then decided to throw it at him to stop him prancing around the room.

After heavy overnight rain, the new day dawned grey and chilly, but a strong, gusty wind was helping to dry out some of the puddles of water lying in every hollow. The brothers ran all the way to the ground, desperate to find out whether the big match was still on or not, and arrived breathless to join a few others already there.

'Lovely and squelchy!' They heard Duggan's voice raised above the rest. 'Little Westy is going to be a real stick in the mud today.'

He was standing in the goalmouth as they approached, the mud oozing over the toes of his wellingtons. There were a few pools of brown water to be seen in the centre circle and both penalty areas, but the state of the pitch down the wings did not seem too bad.

'What do you reckon?' Andrew asked Tim Lawrence, who would have to plough through the mess in midfield more than most.

'Mr Jones told me he thought it was playable if there's no more rain,' Tim replied, 'but the final decision's up to the referee. He's inspecting the pitch now.'

'Are Shenby here yet?' Chris asked.

'Not yet,' Duggan interrupted quickly. 'Getting cold feet, are we?

'No. Just wondered, that's all,' he defended himself.

Even so, he could feel the butterflies churning around inside his stomach with his hurried breakfast. He hated standing about waiting, and he was impatient for things to start happening.

At that moment Mr Jones came across to them. He tried to look as though he had bad news but couldn't keep his face straight as he saw the disappointment in their eyes. 'It's okay, lads,' he grinned at last, 'we're going ahead and hoping for the best.'

They let out a cheer of relief and he had to calm them down again before he could continue. 'It's bound to be tricky underfoot so keep it simple. No fancy stuff near your own goal in this mud. Get the ball away to safety.'

He looked at Chris uneasily. 'Not ideal conditions for your first game, I'm afraid, but good luck. Watch for the ball skidding about. And don't worry, whatever happens, nobody's going to grumble at you if you do make any mistakes.'

Chris shot a glance at the smirking Duggan and felt that this last remark was perhaps not strictly accurate.

'Have you got some gloves?' Mr Jones asked him.

He gulped and avoided Andrew's face. 'Yes,' he said simply.

'Good. You'll certainly be needing them today.'

As he spoke, a convoy of vehicles began to unload a cargo of eager Shenby footballers and Mr Jones went off to welcome them, leaving his own players to troop into the wooden changing hut. Chris felt a gentle nudge on the arm.

'All the best,' whispered Grandad into his ear, and Chris turned in delight. 'Keep your eye on the ball — the wind will be swirling it about this morning.'

'I will, Grandad.'

They grinned at each other and Chris felt reassured, but quickly he was swallowed up inside the noisy, excited atmosphere of the hut, as both teams hurriedly changed.

At last came the moment that he had dreamed of for ages. Mr Jones held out to him the school team goal-keeper's green top with the black figure 1 standing out on the back. The number 1 keeper in the world, he pretended it meant.

'A little earlier than I'd planned,' the headmaster smiled, 'but I'm sure you'll be seeing a lot more of it in time to come.'

The boy clutched his prize lovingly close to his chest as if to prove his dream had indeed come true. 'Thank you,' he murmured.

As soon as he pulled the jersey over his head all nervousness and doubt vanished. He was ready to face anybody. No matter how many more times he might wear it, he knew that he would never forget that first marvellous sensation of feeling its extra padded warmth against his bare skin.

Now he was a real goalkeeper!

He swiftly slipped into his white shorts, tugged on the red socks and laced his boots up tightly. Then, the witch's gloves in one hand, he clattered down the steps out on to the soft, spongy turf. Danebridge's red and white stripes mingled with Shenby's blue shirts as the two sides jogged towards the pitch to warm up. Their bright, freshly-washed kits were not destined to stay those colours for long, however, on such a mud-heap.

The new young goalkeeper spotted his grandad on the touchline giving him an encouraging thumbs-up signal. The importance of the occasion was reflected by the fact that his usual place behind the garden wall was not near enough

today to enjoy his grandson's performance to the full. Chris waved back and then returned the greetings from some of his own friends kicking a ball about just off the pitch.

The fleeting thought entered his head that normally he would have been there with them, playing their own little game and only half watching the main action, but still managing to raise a cheer when Danebridge scored a goal. Today, though, was very different. He knew they would have given anything to be able to swap places with him and actually play for the school team.

Chris forced himself to put them out of his mind and to concentrate on the job in hand. He saw that the goalmouth nearer the River Dane was in a far worse state than the other and realized that the wind was blowing towards it too. Not surprisingly, his spirits sagged a little when the Shenby captain won the toss and indicated he wanted to attack that way first in the hope of gaining an early advantage.

'Just my luck,' he muttered to himself.

Tim Lawrence, though, did not seem to mind. 'Suits us,' he called to his team, clapping his hands to urge them to play well. 'We'll have the wind behind us in the second half when they're tiring.'

He managed a quick word with Andrew. 'Keep the defence tight. We've somehow got to hold on till half-time. Try and give Chris an early

71

feel of the ball, if you can, to settle him down.'

The referee blew his whistle and Chris stood alone in the swampy goal-mouth as the game at last kicked off, his face set with determination to do well.

But his soccer career was fated to get off to a disastrous start. By the time he did get his hands on the ball, Danebridge were already one goal

down in the most tragic manner and there was nothing that he could have done to prevent it.

In Shenby's very first attack, they swept the ball down the right touchline to allow their winger to run at the home side's left-back. Normally the defender would have easily cut out the danger, but as he turned, his feet slithered from underneath him on the greasy surface and his opponent raced past him into the clear.

The winger dribbled into the penalty area and seemed to be trying to set himself up for a shot. Chris was correctly positioned at the near post to block it when, unexpectedly, the ball was hooked hard and low across the face of the goal.

Andrew had been hurtling in to

mark their centre-forward and had no chance to get out of the way of the speeding missile. It struck him on the left knee and flew off wickedly into the top corner of his own goal.

The brothers gaped at each other in horror as Shenby celebrated their lucky success. For Chris, it seemed as though time itself stood still. His feet felt so heavy he could not even move them.

Everything, somehow, faded far away and he felt very small and lonely. His dream-world had caved in around him and the prickle of salty tears stung behind his eyes.

Vaguely, a familiar yet strangely pathetic voice got through to him.

'Sorry, little brother,' he heard it apologize. 'I couldn't help it — honest.'

5 Penalty!

'Forget it, both of you. C'mon, we've got work to do.'

Tim had already fetched the ball and now ruffled Chris's hair to try and cheer him up. 'Nobody's fault,' he continued. 'Let's just get on with the game.'

Similar shouts of encouragement were now floating across from the people on the touchline, but Chris didn't want to look over to where Grandad was standing. He still felt so miserable.

He didn't have much time to gaze around anyway. All too quickly Shenby were threatening his goal again, but this attack broke down and Chris was able to gather up the loose ball and boot it away upfield to get rid of some of his frustration. His first touch had not been a very happy one.

Things almost worsened a minute later when the score nearly became 2-0 after he misjudged a shot completely. He thought he had it covered until the ball dipped in the wind, bounced awkwardly just in front of him and then squirmed through his fingers. With great relief, he saw it swerve to one side and clip the outside of the post instead of going in.

'Good job for you,' came Duggan's angry warning from nearby.

'Leave him alone,' Andrew challenged, 'and let him settle down. He'll be all right. You get back up front and score us a goal.'

'Seems like you're doing all the scoring round here,' Duggan taunted with a sneer, reminding him painfully of his own goal.

Shenby continued to press hard to try and increase their lead. His confidence shattered, Chris fumbled more shots and the whole defence caught his jitters as they panicked and miskicked their clearances.

Added to these troubles on the pitch, Chris became aware of other irritations behind his goal. A couple of older Shenby boys had wandered up and were now deliberately trying to put him off. Their first casual comments were soon followed by jeers and insults at his mistakes, and then they began to throw little chunks of mud in his direction when they thought no-one was looking.

But somebody was.

One piece caught Chris on the back of his neck. 'Pack it up,' he shouted, but that only made them laugh and do it even more. He was at a loss to know how to cope with the situation.

Help arrived, however, before matters got out of hand. Grandad did not normally like to interfere, but today was different. He decided to put a stop to their unfair and unsporting tactics.

'Right! No more of that nonsense, you two,' he announced firmly.

Startled by his sudden appearance

on the scene, the boys did not even attempt to run off and they found themselves being escorted round the pitch, without fuss, to be left in the charge of the Shenby teacher.

Grandad slipped Chris a wink on his way back. 'They won't be bothering you again this match.'

Chris nodded gratefully, and it was straight after this that he made his first decent save when he flung himself low to his right to smother a fierce drive.

That made him feel a whole lot better, and the thud of another shot into the front of his muddy green jersey signalled to his team that at last their keeper had found his form and they could breathe more easily. They had survived the crisis.

But there were still some heart-stopping moments inside the

Danebridge penalty area, as when one inswinging corner flopped into the goalmouth mud to cause a frantic scramble of legs, boots, arms and bodies. The ball cannoned about off players for what seemed like an age, and twice Chris blocked point-blank range efforts without being able to hang on to it. Finally, the confusion was ended when Andrew hacked it right off the line to clear the danger.

'Thanks!' cried Chris in the excitement. 'That makes up for earlier,'

His entire kit was filthy wet by now, but he became almost unrecognizable moments later when he landed full-length, face down, in the largest of the puddles. He stood up, still clutching the ball from his save, with his hair, face and body caked in dark, sticky mud, but grinning widely, his white teeth gleaming through all the dirt. He made a comical sight, but he was loving every minute of being in the thick of the action.

Shenby's pressure paid off, however, with a clever second goal and Chris could do nothing to prevent it. A tricky piece of skill from the left-winger allowed him to jink past two tackles and send an unstoppable shot high over the goalkeeper's head.

In smaller-sized, schoolboy goals it would undoubtedly have sailed over the crossbar as well, but in these it passed comfortably underneath.

There were no nets on the posts and Chris had to recover the ball from the hedge behind, but soon he was smiling again when he watched his opposite number make a similar trip. The visitors' goalkeeper had enjoyed a rather idle first half so far and was caught napping completely by a swift breakaway Danebridge raid seconds before the interval.

It was Tim Lawrence who popped up unmarked in the Shenby area to steer a cross coolly over the line to leave his team only 2-1 down, a well-deserved reward after so much hard work in defence.

Mr Jones was quick to praise everyone at half-time and give them further encouragement. 'The wind's in your favour now in the second half, remember, so go out and show them how to attack.'

He turned to Chris. 'Well played! You've done us proud after a shaky start. But keep on your guard still — it's not over yet.'

It was just as well that Chris did remain alert.

Straight after the re-start the big Shenby centre-forward burst clear for goal with only the keeper to beat. But as he tried to dribble past him, Chris pounced and spread himself down at his feet, grabbing the ball as the attacker sprawled forwards on top of him.

Enjoying the applause, Chris kicked the ball triumphantly away and his brave, important save inspired the whole Danebridge team to put together a series of skilful attacks of their own to prove that they could play good football too.

Even so, it took ten minutes before Shenby cracked, and then they conceded two quick goals.

The equalizer was scored by John

Duggan, challenging strongly as usual in a goalmouth scramble and forcing the ball over the line. Immediately afterwards, with Shenby's defence still disorganized, Tim set off on a thrilling solo run, showing superb balance on the slippery ground. Dancing round several tackles, he cut inside from the right and hit a beauty into the far corner beyond the keeper's desperate dive.

Danebridge suddenly found themselves 3—2 ahead and looked well set for victory.

'You've got 'em on the run now,' one of the fathers called from the touchline. 'Keep it up. Let's have more goals.'

But the boys on the pitch knew it was not as simple as that. Shenby were far from finished. They refused to give in, and in fact the shock of falling behind had seemed to put fresh life into them, as they now charged around in search of the equalizer which would earn them a replay at home.

The Cup match became an exciting end-to-end battle as the teams threw everything they had left at each other and both goals survived several narrow squeaks. Time was rapidly running out, though, for Shenby when they forced Chris to tip the ball round the post for yet another corner and Tim signalled everyone back into the penalty area to protect their slender lead.

The winger played a neat short-corner before whipping the ball across into the box through a great

ruck of bodies. It suddenly loomed up in front of the unsighted Duggan who reacted by blocking it with his hand in panic before a Shenby player could get at it.

As he booted it away, the Shenby team and their supporters were already loudly demanding a penalty for hand-ball and he slumped to the ground in distress.

'It was an accident, I didn't mean to,' he pleaded, shaking his head and failing to find any excuse for his stunned team-mates. 'I don't know why I did it — it just happened . . .'

The referee had no choice, however, but to award a penalty kick and all their hard work seemed to be wasted. Duggan's eyes were not the only ones to be fixed now on goalkeeper

Chris in the desperate hope that he could yet somehow rescue the situation.

John Duggan wished he had not said so many nasty things to him, but it was too late to make up for that now. At least the kid was a good keeper, he had to admit to himself in consolation.

Chris had certainly proved that today to everyone, whatever happened in these next few minutes.

He settled himself on the goal-line, surprised that he felt quite calm considering that everything was at stake and it all seemed to depend upon him. He had never faced a proper penalty like this before and he was not really sure what to expect. The goal around him looked massive and he stared instead at the leather ball, noticing all the dirty marks on it as it sat perched up on the muddy penalty spot a few metres directly in front of him.

The spectators grew hushed in anticipation of the duel, the final shoot-out, and some of the players grouped around the edge of the area hardly dared to watch as the Shenby captain prepared to run in to take the penalty.

Duggan stood, head bowed, hoping for a miracle.

Grandad removed the pipe from his mouth, moistened his lips with his tongue and said a little silent prayer.

Mr Jones wiped his hand nervously down his face as the suspense and tension mounted.

89

But they could do nothing more to help. It was simply all up to Chris.

He crouched on his toes, waiting. Something Grandad once said about saving penalties suddenly flashed into his head: 'Decide which way to dive and do it — don't be tricked into changing your mind.'

He rubbed his gloved hands together to scrape off some of the mud which clung to them, and then decided: he would go left. Somehow, he had to get in the way of it . . .

The whistle sounded in the silence, and the kicker moved confidently in. Wham!

The ball was blasted hard and he dived, almost blindly, to his left. But too far!

His hunch had proved correct, but

the ball had been struck only just left of centre and he felt it smack against his legs.

Chris lay helpless on the ground as it rebounded off him and the screams from the crowd jerked everybody into action.

Duggan's head shot up to see the stranded keeper trying unsuccessfully to scramble to his feet in the slime and the penalty-taker flat out too. He had lost his footing as he kicked the ball and was too dazed at his miss to recover quickly enough.

The ball was spinning crazily right in front of the vacant goal, but it was Andrew who reached it a split second ahead of other lunging feet to whack it out of sight.

The whole Danebridge team mobbed the brothers in sheer delight as the cheers rang out from the touchline.

'I take it all back!' shouted Duggan with huge relief. 'Fantastic save, Westy. Simon wouldn't have smelt it!'

'Just lucky,' Chris tried to say modestly, but his new friend wouldn't accept that.

'Don't talk rubbish. It was magic! Thanks for getting me off the hook.

I'd never have heard the last of it if they'd scored.'

Chris certainly never heard the last of that save. It was talked about for the rest of the season and beyond.

They would probably have kept talking then if Mr Jones had not managed to get their minds back on the game. But for Shenby it had been a cruel blow. Their heads went down and they could not hide their disappointment. They now seemed resigned to defeat and were fortunate, in fact, not to concede another goal before the final whistle blew shortly afterwards.

The Danebridge players celebrated their passage into the next round of the Cup by exchanging the traditional three cheers with Shenby as they gathered together at the end.

'What a game! What a game!' Andrew kept yelling, as he and John Duggan lifted Chris up on to their shoulders to carry him off the field in honour.

As for Chris, he couldn't quite believe it was all happening to him. It seemed almost unreal. But one thing he was sure about. Magic spell or not, the witch's gloves would never see the jumble sale. He would keep them for himself as a souvenir, a secret reminder of this special day as the school team goalkeeper.

Grandad walked back behind the footballers towards the hut with Mr Jones, enjoying their obvious pleasure.

'Thanks for making a young boy

very happy . . . and an old man too,' he said with a chuckle, his eyes wet and shining.

'Not my doing,' the headmaster replied, reflecting the credit back on to Chris. 'He took his big chance with both hands today. He's a hero now. A muddy hero!'

ROB CHILDS

THE BIG PRIZE

Illustrated by Aidan Potts

YOUNG CORGI BOOKS

*With thanks to Kyle and Dan, two
real soccer mascots*

1 Beat-the-Goalie

'Roll up! Roll up!' cried Andrew Weston at the top of his voice. 'Beat-the-Goalie! Score two out of three to win a prize. Roll up!'

'Wish you'd *belt* up,' muttered Chris, his younger brother. 'This isn't a fairground, you know.'

Andrew grinned. 'Got to attract people and earn some cash. Thought that's what we're here for.'

'It is. But just do it quieter, will you? I can't put up with you shouting your head off like that all afternoon.'

Andrew ignored him as usual. 'C'mon, folks, try your luck,' he called out. 'You don't need any skill – the goalie's rubbish!'

Chris threw a football at him, but his brother saw it coming and ducked. 'Missed!' Andrew laughed. 'But I won't. C'mon, I'll be your first

customer and show everybody how easy it is.'

'It'll cost you twenty pence,' Grandad chuckled from his seat nearby.

'What! You're going to charge *me*?'

'Course we are. All for a good cause, remember,' Grandad replied, casting a quick glance over the playing field. He could see there was already quite a crowd jostling around the jumble sale tables. 'Going to be a marvellous day – I can feel it in my old bones.'

Mr Jones, Danebridge Primary School's headmaster, was optimistic too. The February sun was shining kindly on their special Fun Day and he felt very proud of his pupils. The whole event had been their own idea in the first place and they had set up most of the stalls and games themselves.

The children were trying to raise money for extra sports kit and equipment. Not just for the benefit of the school, but also for a local charity which ran a sports club for disabled youngsters.

Matthew Clarke, in his final year at Danebridge, was one of the main organizers of the Fun Day. Mr Jones spotted him now making a bee-line for the Weston family's *Beat-the-Goalie* competition and smiled. He might have guessed it wouldn't take long before soccer-mad Matthew went to have a go at that.

Grandad saw him coming as well. 'Matthew knows what your shooting's like, Andrew,' he joked. 'He's coming to fetch the balls you smack over the bar!'

'No need for him to bother,' Andrew answered confidently. 'They're all gonna end up inside the net.'

'No chance!' Chris scoffed.

'Oh yeah?'

'Yeah!' Although he was two years younger, Chris tried to give back as good as he got. It didn't always work, especially if Andrew lost his temper, but he had learnt to stick up for himself.

Andrew gave him the kind of hard stare that Chris knew so well. This was serious stuff. Andrew meant business. His elder brother's pride was at stake and he carefully placed the ball for the first penalty a few metres in front of the small-sized goal.

Chris crouched on the line, the low crossbar only just above his head. He rubbed his gloved hands down his tracksuit bottoms and got ready to

spring either way as Andrew ran in to shoot.

The young goalie was already good enough to have played twice for Danebridge when the regular school team keeper had been out of action, so he wasn't easily fooled. But he was this time. Chris felt sure that Andrew would blast the ball. That was his big brother's usual penalty-taking method when they played together in the garden.

Chris threw himself to his right, but instead the ball skimmed along the ground into the opposite corner of the goal. Andrew had placed it perfectly with a gentle side-footer. He punched the air in triumph as though he'd scored the winning goal in the F.A. Cup Final.

'Well done, little brother, that was brill. Funniest thing I've seen in years.'

Chris pulled a face. 'You've not won yet. It's two out of three.'

'No trouble,' Andrew smirked, plonking the second ball on the penalty spot. 'So where's this one gonna go, eh?'

'Just shut up and hit it,' Chris replied. He decided to dive to his left, trying to outguess Andrew – but he was wrong again. His heart sank as the ball flashed the other way and then he heard a clunk and Andrew's groan. The shot had clipped the outside of the post and gone wide of the target.

'How lucky can you get?' cried Andrew.

'Must be those lucky gloves of his,' Matthew called out.

'*Lucky* gloves!' Andrew snorted. 'They're just a tatty old pair that should have gone to a jumble sale ages ago.'

'They're witch's gloves,' Chris claimed.

'Rubbish! They belonged to old Mrs Witchell next door, that's all. She's no more a witch than I am.'

Chris shrugged. 'Well, I like to think they've got a magic spell on them. They haven't let me down yet.'

'There's always a first time. You won't even smell this next one.'

Andrew was bored with little side-footers. This was going to be a master-blaster and he took an extra long run-up.

This could go anywhere, Chris said

to himself. Might as well just stay where I am and see what happens.

He did, standing upright in the centre of the goal as Andrew struck the penalty. It sped straight at him like a cannonball, the force of it almost knocking Chris off his feet. He could only parry the ball in self-defence, protecting his face, but it was enough to stop the shot going in.

Andrew lashed the rebound into the net in fury but he knew that it didn't count. There were no second chances in this competition.

Grandad quickly calmed Andrew down. 'Doesn't matter, forget it – everybody's a winner today, especially the charity. Young Chris here will

take some beating in these small goals.'

Andrew nodded and then flashed a grin at his brother. 'I'll have another go at you later,' he promised.

'Fine, and I'll try my luck with you when it's your turn in goal,' Chris replied. 'I've got a feeling this is going to be my lucky day!'

2 *Egg-cellent!*

'Can I have a go now?'

'Sure thing, Matthew,' Chris said. 'As long as you've got twenty pence.'

Matthew Clarke grinned, flipped a coin into the tin and rolled his wheelchair into position. He put the brake on to hold it steady. 'As I can't kick, I'm going to head the balls past you instead.'

'Come in a bit closer, then,' Chris told him. 'The penalty spot's too far away for headers.'

'I'm OK from here. I've been practising.'

Chris never doubted it. They often played together and he knew how keen Matthew was to do well at games. Sometimes Matthew would end up toppling out of the chair in his eagerness to reach the ball first.

Matthew leant back in his seat, took a deep breath and tossed the football up in front of him. The top half of his body then suddenly snapped forward like the spring on a mousetrap. His legs may have been weak but his neck muscles were powerful enough. They sent the ball hurtling from his forehead towards the target.

'Great goal!' cried Andrew from behind the net. 'Right in the top corner.'

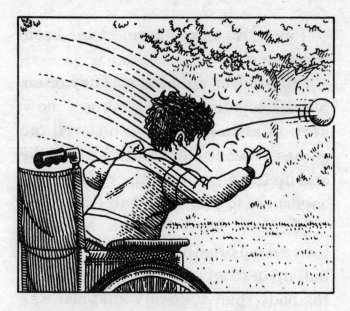

Chris had dived full length but had still been caught out by the speed and accuracy of the header. He missed the next one, too, as Matthew twisted his head round at the last moment and sent the goalkeeper the wrong way.

Andrew was doubled up with laughter. 'Come on, Matt's won already. I'll go in goal for his last effort. Give him a proper contest!'

Chris shrugged and swapped places, exchanging a quick wink with his friend. 'Show him how it's done, Matthew,' he urged.

This time Matthew's body barely moved, but his head suddenly whipped forward with an explosive grunt and the ball flew to the keeper's left. Andrew got a hand to it but could only help the ball into the net.

'Incredible, Matt!' Andrew gasped. 'Had no idea you could head a ball like that. You're better than anybody in our school team.'

Matthew's face was a picture of delight at such praise. 'You ought to see me play wheelchair soccer in the gym with the other disabled kids,' he said. 'I'm the leading scorer.'

'I bet you are,' Andrew laughed. 'I wouldn't like to have to mark you.'

'I'd run you over if you got in my

way,' Matthew grinned. 'I play rough.
I'm always damaging my chair.'

As Matthew tore open the wrap-
ping of his chocolate bar prize, more
of the boys from the charity's sports
club came over to join in. They
attended various schools in and
around the nearby town of Selworth,
but this afternoon they were all the
special guests of Danebridge.
Between them, they kept the brothers
busy for the next hour. Some were
able to kick the ball quite well, a few
threw it and others used their head
like Matthew to try and score. One
even used his crutches.

Chris was in goal most of the time
and allowed everyone to gain some
success against him. If they missed

with both their first two goes, Chris made sure, somehow, that the third went it. His comical 'slips' added to the fun and nobody minded that he wasn't always trying too hard to make a save.

Chris carried on the same way all afternoon. He let little children stand right up to the goal so they could score at least once, but he threw himself about everywhere to stop the shots of people his own age and much older.

Grandad almost purred with pleasure at some of his grandson's saves. Chris was in great form and his performance didn't go unnoticed by others too. Mr Jones, for example. The headmaster knew how much Christopher Weston loved goalkeeping, but it was the boy's sportsmanship that impressed him even more.

All the activities stopped briefly while the main raffle was drawn.

'Green ticket, number twenty-six!' announced Mr Jones loudly. 'A bit early yet for Easter, but our next prize is a giant chocolate egg!'

Chris could hardly believe his eyes. There in his muddy glove lay that very ticket. 'That's me!' he squeaked, his voice cracking in excitement. 'I've won!'

As Chris ran forward to receive the boxed egg, Andrew muttered to one of his pals, 'Typical of our kid's luck, that is, Duggie. He just buys one ticket, and here's me with a fistful and bet I get nothing!'

John Duggan laughed. 'Never mind

the Easter Egg. We're after the star prize today, aren't we?'

'What? In the raffle?'

'Nah!' Duggie sneered. 'You know . . .'

'Oh, yeah, that. Right!' Andrew caught on to what Duggie meant and stared at the man helping the headmaster with the draw. He was Martin North, team captain of Selworth Town Football Club.

The Town had agreed to sponsor the Day's events and several first team players had come along to join in the fun. They had also promised a very special prize of their own.

The players were going to choose one of the pupils to be Selworth's mascot for their next home game in the famous F.A. Cup competition. And that lucky person would have the honour of running out in front of the team, wearing a free souvenir kit in the Club's colours.

Duggie, like the rest of the Danebridge soccer squad, was desperate to catch their eye. 'North's already seen me doing a bit of ball juggling,' he boasted. 'Said I was good, too. Must be in with a chance of being picked.'

'Sorry! He'll forget all about you when he gets over to our game and sees me in action,' Andrew taunted him.

Chris, too, had dreamt of being chosen as mascot. But for the moment at least, he was more than happy with his huge Easter Egg. He put it in the corner of the net for safe-keeping.

And he would soon need to be a safe keeper to protect it – Martin North and Dave Adams, Selworth's top goalscorer and chief penalty-taker, were heading their way!

The brothers saw them early, still surrounded by a pack of autograph hunters, but not as early as Duggie.

'C'mon, little Westy,' he called out. 'My turn. I'm gonna show you – and them – how penalties should be taken.'

Chris sighed. Duggie could be such a big-head at times. He always wanted to prove how good he was at scoring goals and loved nothing better than hammering the ball past him into the net.

Chris braced himself as the striker ran in but barely had time to move. The ball smashed against the cross-bar and spun up into the air before he could even blink.

Duggie threw his hands up in horror, but struck the next one just as hard. He managed to keep this one low but it was too near the goalie. The ball rebounded off Chris's knee to safety, the force of it making him hobble around for a few moments as he rubbed the sore spot.

'The talent-spotters won't think much of that effort, Duggie!' Andrew chortled. 'Last go coming up.'

Frustrated, Duggie charged in again and Chris this time decided to dive out of the way of the missile. But as he did, there was a sickening crunch behind him. He had forgotten about the egg! The ball had scored a direct hit on the box, buckling it up and bursting the packaging.

Everyone gathered round to inspect the damage, hushed at first until they sensed that Chris saw the funny side of it too. Then the jokes came.

'An *egg-cellent* shot, Duggie, my old mate!' whooped Andrew.

'Yeah, thanks to my *egg-stra* power!' cackled Duggie.

Generously, Chris began to share out the broken pieces of chocolate. 'Might as well eat it all now, I guess,' he smiled.

'Good old Duggie!' laughed Matthew. 'Couldn't have aimed it better myself. A fine *egg-sample* of penalty-taking!'

3   *Star Prize*

When the two Selworth Town players finally arrived on the scene, it wasn't just shyness that prevented the boys from speaking at first. Their mouths were still full of chocolate.

Chris at last found his voice. 'Er, sorry, we don't seem to have any Easter Egg left to offer you. It's all gone.'

The men laughed. 'So we see,' said Martin North. 'Not to worry. Dave here wants to try and win a bar of

chocolate instead for himself. You the keeper?'

Chris nodded, hardly able to believe he was about to face Dave Adams, Selworth's star striker.

'Right, then, in goal and let's see if Dave can put any past you.'

Quite a crowd gathered round to watch the big shoot-out, the other lads full of envy. They would have given anything to be in Chris's boots right now. Or even in his 'lucky' gloves . . .

He was beaten for pace by Adams's first penalty but the ball struck the inside of the post. It flew across the goal-line, hit the other post and bounced straight back into Chris's waiting arms. He stood there hugging the ball and grinning like a chimp at a tea-party.

Adams tried again, but Chris this time didn't need any help from the woodwork. He pulled off a wonder-save, finger-tipping the ball just over the bar to earn even louder cheers than before.

The Selworth winger shook his head in amazement. 'I just can't beat this guy!' Adams cried out, attempting to cover his embarrassment with a laugh. 'Sign him up, somebody – he can come and play for us!'

'One left, Dave,' the captain reminded his teammate jokily. 'Miss this and you won't be able to show your face in the dressing-room again. We'll have to sell you!'

He did miss it. He took extra careful aim because of the small-sized goal

and was clever enough to send the boy the wrong way. But Chris still managed to block the shot with his outstretched leg and keep it out.

'Fantastic!' Matthew yelled as Chris found himself mobbed. 'You're a real star now!'

Andrew leant on the goalpost, jealous of Chris's sudden new fame. The way Andrew had pictured it, this sort of thing was supposed to be happening to him, not his kid brother.

The Selworth captain now had to step forward to save the Club's reputation and Chris's luck didn't quite last out. North scored twice, but not before Chris had pushed his first effort against the post.

The Fun Day proved a great success, raising more money for the school and the charity than they had ever expected. Right at the end, after presenting a cheque from Selworth Town F.C., North announced their decision.

'We've seen some very promising sporting talent here this afternoon, but one boy for us has really stood out. Not even our best penalty-taker could beat him.'

The player paused as everyone looked round at a red-faced Chris. 'And with his kind of luck,' North continued, 'winning that Easter Egg too, he's got to be our choice for team mascot in the F.A. Cup.'

Chris was pushed up to the front through the crowd to shake Martin North's hand. 'Here he is,' the captain greeted him. 'A big round of applause,

please, for Christopher Weston, a very *egg-cited* young man!'

Danebridge School had a cup-tie of their own first, a quarter-final match away from home. Chris went to watch Andrew play as usual and invited Matthew to come, too, his wheelchair folded and strapped to the roof-rack of Grandad's car.

Matthew tried to support the school team as often as he could, cheering himself silly from his chair. As far as he was concerned, it was the next best thing to being out on the pitch, running around with his pals.

He knew he would never be able to do that. But thanks to the fund-raising, the charity could now start to provide more chances for him and others like him to enjoy their various wheelchair sports such as soccer and basketball.

As Chris pushed him along towards the touchline, Matthew said, 'You ought to be playing today, after what you did in goal on the Fun Day.'

'Simon Garner's still first choice,' Chris replied. 'He's older.'

'Not better, though.'

'Well, thanks, but Simon's a pretty good keeper really.'

Matthew giggled. 'He's not as good as you at saving penalties!'

'Let's just hope he doesn't have to face any today, then,' Chris said as the two teams jogged out on to the pitch.

Tim Lawrence, the Danebridge skipper, won the toss and decided to kick first into the strong breeze.

'Tim always prefers to have the wind behind him in the second half when everyone's a bit tired,' Matthew explained. 'But if it was me, I'd use the wind straightaway.'

'Why's that?' asked Chris.

'Try to go a few goals up early on and hope the other lot give in.'

Chris nodded. 'What do you think, Grandad?'

'Makes sense,' he agreed, struggling to light his pipe in the wind. 'There was one game I played as a kid – howling gale, it was. So strong, we could hardly get the ball out of our own penalty area. Six–nil down at half-time, we were, but reckoned we'd get our own back in the second half.'

'What happened?'

'Ended up losing ten–nil,' Grandad chuckled. 'Pesky wind went and died

down all of a sudden when we changed round, just like somebody had gone and switched it off!'

'How do you remember the score after all this time?' Matthew asked.

Grandad gave Chris a wink. His grandson already knew the answer. 'I was in goal, lad, that's why. Only time in my life I let in double figures! Goalies always remember bad days like that.'

4 One of Those Days

There was no danger this game of Simon Garner suffering the same fate as Grandad.

Although Danebridge were forced to defend for much of the first half, Simon had not been especially busy. Andrew at centre-back had the defence well organized. Most of the home side's attacks broke down before getting a clear sight of goal.

Then, on a rare raid, Duggie raced away to shoot Danebridge ahead and they looked well set up for an easy win in the second half. But by the time the referee blew for the interval, they were 2–1 down instead. Both goals came in the space of three minutes.

The equalizer was a disaster. Andrew was certain the attacker was offside, but even so, his shot was a tame one. Simon seemed to have it well covered until somehow he let the ball squirm from his grasp and slip over the line.

Simon's error gave him the jitters. He soon fumbled another shot and Andrew had to hook the ball out of play. It only delayed the second goal briefly. The nervous keeper couldn't hold the corner and saw the ball lashed back past him into the roof of the net.

'Sorry!' Simon apologized to his teammates as they gathered round Mr Jones at the interval.

'Forget about it, Simon,' the headmaster said. 'Everybody makes mistakes. I don't expect you to have much to do now with the wind in our favour. Let's work hard, lads, to keep the ball in their half.'

They did just that. Simon was little more than a spectator and watched his team first draw level and then go in front. In the end, to his great relief, Danebridge ran up a 4–2 lead which was enough to see them safely through to the semi-finals.

'I could have played in goal second half and it wouldn't have made any difference,' Matthew joked as he and Chris waited for the teams to change afterwards.

Chris was tossing a ball to him to

head back when the headmaster came out of the school building and saw them. 'Enjoy the match, lads?'

They nodded and Mr Jones then spoke directly to Chris. 'Fancy a bit of a game yourself next week, do you?'

Chris jumped at the chance to play for the school again.

'Good,' said Mr Jones. 'Knew you'd be pleased. I'd like to give you some more experience and it'll help to keep Simon on his toes, knowing you're around. I'll give you half a game each.'

As the headmaster went off, Matthew said, 'Lucky old you. You know what that game is, don't you?'

Chris shook his head.

'It's a vital league match. Bet he's hoping that some of your luck will rub off on the team. We'll need it, too. We're playing Hanfield and they're top of the league.'

Grandad butted in. 'It's also the same day, remember, when you're due to be Selworth's mascot.'

'Wow!' Matthew whistled. 'Playing in the morning, mascot in the afternoon. What a day! Hope those gloves of yours keep working their magic!'

'Can't wait till this afternoon!'

The week had dragged by so slowly for Chris. His mind kept drifting away to the excitement that lay ahead, and he'd been told off in class many times for day-dreaming. 'Just think,' he babbled on. 'Little me trotting out with the Selworth team in front of all those people!'

He was trying to keep up with his older brother as they jogged towards the village recreation ground for the school's league match.

Suddenly Andrew stopped and turned on him. 'Look, you've been going on all week about not being able to wait till Saturday. Now it's here, you start on about this afternoon. We've got a big game ourselves this morning first, never mind Selworth.'

'I know, I know,' Chris replied. 'But hardly the F.A. Cup, is it?'

'So? It's just as important to us. We've got to beat Hanfield to stand any chance of winning the league championship.'

'I'll be doing my best, don't worry.'

'Just see that you do,' Andrew said gruffly. 'We can't afford to have any slip-ups today.'

Sadly, however, when Chris made his promised appearance after half-time, Danebridge were already trailing 2–1, just as in the previous game. And once again, Simon had not had the happiest of times. After Tim had equalized Hanfield's early opening goal, Simon was slow to get down to a low skimming shot and let the ball bobble under his body.

The goalkeeper hung his head in dismay, not wanting to catch anybody's eye. The kind of form he was in, he would probably have dropped it anyway!

Watching from the garden wall of his cottage next to the recky pitch, Grandad gave Chris the thumbs-up sign. Chris returned it and tugged nervously on his 'lucky' gloves. He so much wanted to do well. A good performance today and he might even keep Simon out of the team. Thoughts about his mascot duties somehow had to be forgotten, at least for the moment.

Despite being behind, Danebridge started the half in bright fashion. They put together a couple of dangerous attacks, forcing the other goalkeeper to make two good saves. A second equalizer looked likely until a Hanfield striker broke loose and sprinted clear of Andrew and the rest of the defence.

Chris came out to meet him but the attacker wasn't to be panicked into shooting wildly. He stayed calm and tried to dribble round the keeper. Chris lunged at the ball just as the boy whisked it away out of reach and then fell as Chris's arm caught his leg and brought him down.

'Penalty!' screamed all the

Hanfield team and supporters. Mr Jones, the referee, reluctantly had to agree.

'You great wally!' cried Andrew, standing over his brother. 'What did you go and do a clumsy thing like that for?'

'I didn't mean to,' Chris defended himself. 'It just happened.'

'There was no need to charge out of goal like that. I'd have caught him up before he shot.'

Chris knew that wasn't true but had no chance to argue.

'Don't get at each other, you two,' Mr Jones ordered. 'That doesn't help matters at all.'

Andrew still had the last word. 'Right, little brother, if you're so brilliant at saving penalties, make up for it by stopping this one.'

'C'mon, Chris,' Matthew shouted from the touchline. 'You show 'em. Remember Dave Adams!'

Chris frowned. This, he knew, was a completely different situation. For a start, the recky goal was huge, and this was for real, not for a bit of fun.

Waiting on the goal-line, Chris watched the penalty-taker run in. The boy tried to disguise which way he was going to place the kick, but Chris guessed correctly. He threw himself to the right but the ball was well struck – hard and high. Chris felt it brush past his fingers and then heard the sound that all goalkeepers dread and all goalscorers love. The

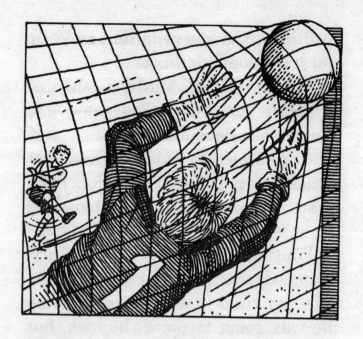

swish of the football hitting the back of the netting.

Danebridge were now 3–1 behind and their dreams of the league title were disappearing fast in the cold light of day.

Duggie, for one, was not about to give up, however. He soon shocked the league leaders with a superb headed goal from a corner and sent another shot only a fraction wide.

But the brave fightback was halted in its tracks. Chris blocked one effort during a goalmouth scramble, and was unable to keep hold of the ball again when it was driven at him through a crowd of bodies. It popped out of his gloves and a Hanfield player finally forced it over the line to put them two goals ahead once more.

Duggie fished the ball out the net and couldn't resist a dig at the miserable young goalkeeper before he hurried back upfield to kick off. 'Huh! Some *lucky* mascot you're gonna be – Selworth have got no chance this afternoon with *you* around!'

5 Lucky Mascot?

Duggie's taunt stung Chris. He ripped off his 'lucky' witch's gloves and threw them into the back of the net.

'Never going to wear those useless things again. They don't give me enough grip. Wish I'd worn my proper goalie gloves.'

Andrew was unsympathetic. 'We've got no chance now, thanks to you.'

'That's not fair. You were losing even before I came on.'

'Yeah, and you've gone and made it worse.'

'Anybody can have an off day,' muttered Chris.

'True,' Andrew sneered, 'but why did you choose this one?'

Chris pulled a face. The special day had not started quite the way he'd hoped. At this rate, his teammates would probably jeer rather than cheer him when he took the field with Selworth that afternoon.

Hanfield played with more and more confidence now with a cushion of a two-goal lead and set about increasing it further. Not even Tim and Duggie could work any miracles to get Danebridge back into the game.

Chris was kept too busy to worry any more about his earlier errors. He began to show his true abilities, catching the ball cleanly with his bare hands and making two outstanding saves. But all in vain. The damage had already been done – at least in terms of dashing the school's hopes of winning the league title.

For Chris, unfortunately, the real damage was still to come. As the game entered the last minute, Hanfield mounted yet another attack.

The ball was swept across into the goalmouth, Andrew headed it away, but straight to a player lurking outside the area. He hammered it back in on the volley beautifully. Chris made a move for the ball, but then saw it take a massive deflection off a Danebridge leg. He had to twist back suddenly in the opposite direction.

'Ow!' His ankle gave way underneath him and he yelped in pain. He sank to the ground as the ball looped into the net for Hanfield's fifth goal but Chris was past caring. His ankle felt like it was on fire.

Helping hands tried to lift him up. 'It's almost the end, Chris,' said Mr Jones. 'Can you carry on?'

The boy shook his head, forcing back the tears. He couldn't even stand up by himself. Then he heard

Grandad's voice. He hadn't seen that Grandad was already at his side.

Forgetting his age, Grandad had run across the pitch as soon as he realized that Chris was hurt. 'C'mon, my lad. Game's over for you. You're back to the cottage with me for some first aid. Bring his gear with you later, Andrew.'

Another spectator helped carry Chris off and into Grandad's kitchen while Andrew himself pulled on the green goalie top. When he reported back to the cottage after the match, joking that he'd kept a clean sheet, he found Chris with his foot wrapped up in a cold, wet towel.

'What's that for?' asked Andrew.

'Grandad's trying to prevent too

much swelling,' Chris said, wincing as Andrew bent to touch his ankle. 'Don't do that. I've twisted it.'

'Tough luck, our kid,' Andrew said, attempting to keep a straight face. 'What about this afternoon, then?'

Chris sighed heavily and shook his head. 'Dunno yet. Don't see how I can make it now I've done this. Can't really go crawling out in front of the team on my hands and knees, can I?'

Andrew smirked. 'I could always take your place.'

'Oh, yeah, you'd like that, wouldn't you? Leave me here suffering while you go off and hog all the glory for yourself.'

Andrew shrugged. 'Just a thought. Somebody's got to go and do it. Can't leave the Town without a mascot for their big cup match.'

That same terrible thought had been occupying Chris's mind ever since his injury. 'Looks like it's not going to be my day after all,' he groaned. 'Sorry about the goals I let in.'

Andrew shrugged. 'Doubt if we'd have beaten them anyway. Have to admit, they were a bit too good for us.'

There was a knock at Grandad's front door and in rolled Matthew in his wheelchair. 'Couldn't reach up to the bell,' he grinned. 'Thought I'd better come and see if I could do anything to help.'

By school minibus and cars, the Danebridge soccer squad arrived at Selworth stadium's main car-park in good time before the match. The Club

had given them all free grandstand tickets and the treat helped to make up for their own disappointment earlier.

Grandad took Matthew's wheel-chair down from the roof-rack and Andrew began to help its user from the back seat of the car.

'I can manage. I'm not completely helpless, you know.'

Andrew laughed. 'OK, I'll just stand here and watch you struggle.'

Feeling everybody was watching him, the invalid hopped clumsily across the small gap and slumped into the chair. 'Made it, you see.'

'Sure! I can just see you trying to hop about all over the pitch!'

Chris smiled at the thought and gave up. 'OK, you win, I do need some help. Give me a push. I haven't got the hang of this thing yet.'

'Nor these!' added Grandad, tucking a pair of crutches under his arm. 'But you're going to need them in a bit, if you're wanting to go and meet the players down in the dressing-room.'

'Yeah!' Andrew agreed. 'No way am I going to lug you up and down any steps in Matt's wheelchair.'

Matthew Clarke had come to Chris's rescue. He would be at the match himself as usual, sitting in the area reserved for disabled spectators, but had offered to lend Chris his crutches and spare wheelchair.

Chris hadn't really fancied the idea, but Grandad and Andrew talked him into trying it. 'It's the only way you'll manage this afternoon with that bad ankle of yours,' Grandad told him. 'You've got to keep your weight off it for a while.'

'I'll feel stupid,' said Chris.

'You *are* stupid, getting yourself injured on a day like this,' Andrew replied. 'But it's either the chair or me taking your place. Take your pick!'

The wheelchair won but Andrew got his wish too. He was planning to

push Chris out on to the pitch himself!

'This has got to be some kind of joke!' Dave Adams cried when Chris wobbled into the dressing-room, his ankle heavily strapped up with bandages. 'I've been telling everyone that this kid who saved all my penalties was dead lucky – and then he goes and turns up on crutches!'

The players laughed at their teammate and listened with amusement as Grandad told them Chris's tale of woe.

'Great omen for the match, this is, lads, eh?' smiled the captain, giving Chris a wink. 'Even our lucky mascot's gone lame!'

6   Catch!

The roar from the packed crowd was deafening. As soon as the home team were spotted coming out of the players' tunnel, the chants and the cheers trebled in volume.

Then, for a moment, the sound died as the spectators looked more closely. Leading Selworth out on to the pitch was a lad in a wheelchair, kitted out as a goalkeeper and pushed by an older boy wearing a tracksuit. It wasn't exactly the sight they had been expecting!

The brothers were stunned by the noise. 'This is amazing!' cried Andrew, slapping Chris on his shoulder. 'Fantastic feeling!'

Chris could hardly hear him, but he was just as excited. He completely forgot about his nervousness and embarrassment in the thrill of the moment. He would dearly have loved to run out with the team properly, but at least being pushed was the next best thing.

As the players began to warm up at their favourite end of the ground in front of their fans, Andrew wheeled Chris towards the penalty area. Chris had promised to look out for Matthew near the corner flag and now saw him waving madly.

Chris had a bit of trouble waving back as he was trying to balance the crutches across the arms of the chair as well. He told Andrew to stop. 'Put the brake on. This is where I get off,' he shouted.

If anything, the crowd's cheers seemed to become even louder as Andrew helped his brother to stand up on the crutches and totter towards the goal. They were clearly enjoying the boy's spirited efforts to join in. Chris bashed at the ball with one of his crutches, and then with Andrew holding on to him, he unwisely attempted to kick at goal.

'Not with your bad foot,' Andrew reminded him.

His left ankle was still too sore

to put on the ground. Chris tried to balance briefly on the crutches and swing his right boot at the ball. He made contact, but lost his balance altogether and fell down in an untidy heap to hoots of laughter from the crowd.

Chris no longer minded. He was enjoying himself, too, being at the centre of all the fuss and attention. The Selworth goalkeeper helped Andrew lift the mascot back into the wheelchair.

'Safest place for you, I reckon,' the man grinned. 'You'll only make the injury worse fooling about on it. You sit there and I'll lob a few balls at you to catch, OK?'

'Great!' Chris cried. He didn't drop a single ball and received a loud cheer for every catch.

Andrew, meanwhile, cheekily took

the chance to whack a loose football into the unguarded net. 'What a goal!' he shouted and then realized the captains were being called to the centre-circle to toss up.

He ran back to the wheelchair. 'C'mon, you're needed,' he cried. 'Cor! This is getting hard work, pushing you. Why won't this thing go? Is it stuck in the mud or something?'

'It helps if you take the brake off first,' Chris suggested.

Andrew stood to one side to let Chris have the honour by himself of shaking hands with both captains and the referee. After the toss, Chris was given the coin as a souvenir and he posed for the press photographer with the players – and Andrew, too, when Martin North invited him to join the group.

Then, far too quickly, it was all over. The match was about to kick off and the mascot's brief moments in the limelight were at an end.

'Time to clear off,' Andrew said as he wheeled Chris back towards the touchline. 'Duty done – now the real business is about to start.'

'I'm still their mascot,' Chris protested. 'I've still got to try and bring them good luck.'

'I think you used up all your luck at the Fun Day,' Andrew replied.

The Club had found places near the trainers' benches beside the pitch for Grandad and the brothers. It was too difficult for Chris to reach the rest of the Danebridge party up in the stands.

'Magic! Right up close to the action,' Chris called out above the noise as the cup-tie got under way. 'I'm still lucky, you see, Andrew, getting us front row seats like this.'

Andrew grinned. 'Feels like we're almost playing. Might even have a kick or two if the ball comes out of play near us.'

Much to Andrew's regret, the ball never did come their way until near the end. By which time, the game was locked in stalemate and seemed set to be a goal-less draw.

A replay at home was obviously what the visiting team were hoping for. And they looked like achieving it, too, until Selworth's lucky mascot played a hand. Both hands, in fact.

The visitors were being jeered for their time-wasting tactics when, once again, the ball was booted aimlessly out of play for a throw-in.

As it flew over his head, Chris's natural goalkeeping instincts took over. He forgot all about his bad ankle. He leapt up from his seat to pluck the ball cleanly out of the air before it disappeared into the crowd behind him.

North charged up, demanding the ball, and Chris swiftly tossed it to him. Selworth's opponents had briefly relaxed when the ball went out and the quick throw-in caught them off guard.

The captain's accurate throw found Dave Adams unmarked and the star striker raced clear for goal. Adams

Grandad chuckled with pride. 'He might only have one leg to stand on right now, but all a good keeper needs is two safe hands!'

'And a bit of luck,' Chris added happily.

'Aye, that helps, too,' Grandad smiled. 'But good players always make their own luck, m'boy, and don't you ever forget it!'

THE END

made no mistake. He drew the goal-keeper out, nipped skilfully round him and slotted the ball into the empty net. The crowd went wild with excitement.

'The winner!' screamed Andrew. 'Got to be!'

The Selworth players felt sure too. Many of them rushed across to Chris as part of their celebrations to ruffle his mop of fair hair.

'Great stuff, kid!' cried Adams. 'Told 'em you were lucky!'

After the referee blew the final whistle, Martin North came over to slap Chris on the back. 'We're through to the next round, thanks to you. We'd never have scored if you hadn't made that brilliant catch.'